MUAMMAR EL-QADDAFI

WORLD LEADERS PAST & PRESENT

MUAMMAR EL-QADDAFI

Benjamin Kyle

CHELSEA HOUSE PUBLISHERS
NEW YORK
NEW HAVEN PHILADELPHIA

EDITORIAL DIRECTOR: Nancy Toff
MANAGING EDITOR: Karyn Gullen Browne
COPY CHIEF: Perry Scott King
ART DIRECTOR: Giannella Garrett
PICTURE EDITOR: Elizabeth Terhune

Staff for MUAMMAR EL-QADDAFI

SENIOR EDITOR: John W. Selfridge
ASSISTANT EDITORS: Maria Behan, Pierre Hauser, Howard Ratner, Bert Yaeger
COPY EDITORS: Sean Dolan, Kathleen McDermott
DESIGN ASSISTANT: Jill Goldreyer
PICTURE RESEARCH: Karen Herman
LAYOUT: Irene Friedman
PRODUCTION COORDINATOR: Alma Rodriguez
PRODUCTION ASSISTANT: Karen Dreste
COVER ILLUSTRATION: Richard Leonard

CREATIVE DIRECTOR: Harold Steinberg

Frontispiece courtesy of UPI/Bettmann Photos

3 5 7 9 8 6 4

Library of Congress Cataloging in Publication Data

Kyle, Benjamin. MUAMMAR EL-QADDAFI

(World leaders past & present)
Bibliography: p.
Includes index.
1. Qaddafi, Muammar—Juvenile literature. 2. Libya—Presidents—Biography—Juvenile literature. 3. Heads of state—Libya—Juvenile literature. [1. Qaddafi, Muammar. 2. Heads of state] I. Title. II. Series.
DT236.Q26K94 1987 961'.204'0924 [B] [92] 86-31011

ISBN 0-87754-598-7

Contents

John Adams
John Quincy Adams
Konrad Adenauer
Alexander the Great
Salvador Allende
Marc Antony
Corazon Aquino
Yasir Arafat
King Arthur
Hafez al-Assad
Kemal Atatürk
Attila
Clement Attlee
Augustus Caesar
Menachem Begin
David Ben-Gurion
Otto von Bismarck
Léon Blum
Simon Bolívar
Cesare Borgia
Willy Brandt
Leonid Brezhnev
Julius Caesar
John Calvin
Jimmy Carter
Fidel Castro
Catherine the Great
Charlemagne
Chiang Kai-Shek
Winston Churchill
Georges Clemenceau
Cleopatra
Constantine the Great
Hernán Cortés
Oliver Cromwell
Georges-Jacques Danton
Jefferson Davis
Moshe Dayan
Charles de Gaulle
Eamon De Valera
Eugene Debs
Deng Xiaoping
Benjamin Disraeli
Alexander Dubček
François & Jean-Claude Duvalier
Dwight Eisenhower
Eleanor of Aquitaine
Elizabeth I
Faisal
Ferdinand & Isabella
Francisco Franco
Benjamin Franklin
Frederick the Great
Indira Gandhi
Mohandas Gandhi
Giuseppe Garibaldi
Amin & Bashir Gemayel
Genghis Khan
William Gladstone
Mikhail Gorbachev
Ulysses S. Grant
Ernesto "Che" Guevara
Tenzin Gyatso
Alexander Hamilton
Dag Hammarskjöld
Henry VIII
Henry of Navarre
Paul von Hindenburg
Hirohito
Adolf Hitler
Ho Chi Minh
King Hussein
Ivan the Terrible
Andrew Jackson
James I
Wojciech Jaruzelski
Thomas Jefferson
Joan of Arc
Pope John XXIII
Pope John Paul II
Lyndon Johnson
Benito Juárez
John Kennedy
Robert Kennedy
Jomo Kenyatta
Ayatollah Khomeini
Nikita Khrushchev
Kim Il Sung
Martin Luther King, Jr.
Henry Kissinger
Kublai Khan
Lafayette
Robert E. Lee
Vladimir Lenin
Abraham Lincoln
David Lloyd George
Louis XIV
Martin Luther
Judas Maccabeus
James Madison
Nelson & Winnie Mandela
Mao Zedong
Ferdinand Marcos
George Marshall
Mary, Queen of Scots
Tomáš Masaryk
Golda Meir
Klemens von Metternich
James Monroe
Hosni Mubarak
Robert Mugabe
Benito Mussolini
Napoléon Bonaparte
Gamal Abdel Nasser
Jawaharlal Nehru
Nero
Nicholas II
Richard Nixon
Kwame Nkrumah
Daniel Ortega
Mohammed Reza Pahlavi
Thomas Paine
Charles Stewart Parnell
Pericles
Juan Perón
Peter the Great
Pol Pot
Muammar el-Qaddafi
Ronald Reagan
Cardinal Richelieu
Maximilien Robespierre
Eleanor Roosevelt
Franklin Roosevelt
Theodore Roosevelt
Anwar Sadat
Haile Selassie
Prince Sihanouk
Jan Smuts
Joseph Stalin
Sukarno
Sun Yat-sen
Tamerlane
Mother Teresa
Margaret Thatcher
Josip Broz Tito
Toussaint L'Ouverture
Leon Trotsky
Pierre Trudeau
Harry Truman
Queen Victoria
Lech Walesa
George Washington
Chaim Weizmann
Woodrow Wilson
Xerxes
Emiliano Zapata
Zhou Enlai

ON LEADERSHIP

Arthur M. Schlesinger, jr.

LEADERSHIP, it may be said, is really what makes the world go round. Love no doubt smooths the passage; but love is a private transaction between consenting adults. Leadership is a public transaction with history. The idea of leadership affirms the capacity of individuals to move, inspire, and mobilize masses of people so that they act together in pursuit of an end. Sometimes leadership serves good purposes, sometimes bad; but whether the end is benign or evil, great leaders are those men and women who leave their personal stamp on history.

Now, the very concept of leadership implies the proposition that individuals can make a difference. This proposition has never been universally accepted. From classical times to the present day, eminent thinkers have regarded individuals as no more than the agents and pawns of larger forces, whether the gods and goddesses of the ancient world or, in the modern era, race, class, nation, the dialectic, the will of the people, the spirit of the times, history itself. Against such forces, the individual dwindles into insignificance.

So contends the thesis of historical determinism. Tolstoy's great novel *War and Peace* offers a famous statement of the case. Why, Tolstoy asked, did millions of men in the Napoleonic Wars, denying their human feelings and their common sense, move back and forth across Europe slaughtering their fellows? "The war," Tolstoy answered, "was bound to happen simply because it was bound to happen." All prior history predetermined it. As for leaders, they, Tolstoy said, "are but the labels that serve to give a name to an end and, like labels, they have the least possible connection with the event." The greater the leader, "the more conspicuous the inevitability and the predestination of every act he commits." The leader, said Tolstoy, is "the slave of history."

Determinism takes many forms. Marxism is the determinism of class. Nazism the determinism of race. But the idea of men and women as the slaves of history runs athwart the deepest human instincts. Rigid determinism abolishes the idea of human freedom—

the assumption of free choice that underlies every move we make, every word we speak, every thought we think. It abolishes the idea of human responsibility, since it is manifestly unfair to reward or punish people for actions that are by definition beyond their control. No one can live consistently by any deterministic creed. The Marxist states prove this themselves by their extreme susceptibility to the cult of leadership.

More than that, history refutes the idea that individuals make no difference. In December 1931 a British politician crossing Park Avenue in New York City between 76th and 77th Streets around 10:30 P.M. looked in the wrong direction and was knocked down by an automobile—a moment, he later recalled, of a man aghast, a world aglare: "I do not understand why I was not broken like an eggshell or squashed like a gooseberry." Fourteen months later an American politician, sitting in an open car in Miami, Florida, was fired on by an assassin; the man beside him was hit. Those who believe that individuals make no difference to history might well ponder whether the next two decades would have been the same had Mario Constasino's car killed Winston Churchill in 1931 and Giuseppe Zangara's bullet killed Franklin Roosevelt in 1933. Suppose, in addition, that Adolf Hitler had been killed in the street fighting during the Munich *Putsch* of 1923 and that Lenin had died of typhus during World War I. What would the 20th century be like now?

For better or for worse, individuals do make a difference. "The notion that a people can run itself and its affairs anonymously," wrote the philosopher William James, "is now well known to be the silliest of absurdities. Mankind does nothing save through initiatives on the part of inventors, great or small, and imitation by the rest of us—these are the sole factors in human progress. Individuals of genius show the way, and set the patterns, which common people then adopt and follow."

Leadership, James suggests, means leadership in thought as well as in action. In the long run, leaders in thought may well make the greater difference to the world. But, as Woodrow Wilson once said, "Those only are leaders of men, in the general eye, who lead in action. . . . It is at their hands that new thought gets its translation into the crude language of deeds." Leaders in thought often invent in solitude and obscurity, leaving to later generations the tasks of imitation. Leaders in action—the leaders portrayed in this series—have to be effective in their own time.

And they cannot be effective by themselves. They must act in response to the rhythms of their age. Their genius must be adapted, in a phrase of William James's, "to the receptivities of the moment." Leaders are useless without followers. "There goes the mob," said the French politician hearing a clamor in the streets. "I am their leader. I must follow them." Great leaders turn the inchoate emotions of the mob to purposes of their own. They seize on the opportunities of their time, the hopes, fears, frustrations, crises, potentialities. They succeed when events have prepared the way for them, when the community is awaiting to be aroused, when they can provide the clarifying and organizing ideas. Leadership ignites the circuit between the individual and the mass and thereby alters history.

It may alter history for better or for worse. Leaders have been responsible for the most extravagant follies and most monstrous crimes that have beset suffering humanity. They have also been vital in such gains as humanity has made in individual freedom, religious and racial tolerance, social justice, and respect for human rights.

There is no sure way to tell in advance who is going to lead for good and who for evil. But a glance at the gallery of men and women in *World Leaders—Past and Present* suggests some useful tests.

One test is this: Do leaders lead by force or by persuasion? By command or by consent? Through most of history leadership was exercised by the divine right of authority. The duty of followers was to defer and to obey. "Theirs not to reason why / Theirs but to do and die." On occasion, as with the so-called enlightened despots of the 18th century in Europe, absolutist leadership was animated by humane purposes. More often, absolutism nourished the passion for domination, land, gold, and conquest and resulted in tyranny.

The great revolution of modern times has been the revolution of equality. The idea that all people should be equal in their legal condition has undermined the old structure of authority, hierarchy, and deference. The revolution of equality has had two contrary effects on the nature of leadership. For equality, as Alexis de Tocqueville pointed out in his great study *Democracy in America,* might mean equality in servitude as well as equality in freedom.

"I know of only two methods of establishing equality in the political world," Tocqueville wrote. "Rights must be given to every citizen, or none at all to anyone . . . save one, who is the master of all." There was no middle ground "between the sovereignty of all and the absolute power of one man." In his astonishing prediction of 20th-century totalitarian dictatorship, Tocqueville explained how the revolution of equality could lead to the *"Führerprinzip"* and more terrible absolutism than the world had ever known.

But when rights are given to every citizen and the sovereignty of all is established, the problem of leadership takes a new form, becomes more exacting than ever before. It is easy to issue commands and enforce them by the rope and the stake, the concentration camp and the *gulag.* It is much harder to use argument and achievement to overcome opposition and win consent. The Founding Fathers of the United States understood the difficulty. They believed that history had given them the opportunity to decide, as Alexander Hamilton wrote in the first Federalist Paper, whether men are indeed capable of basing government on "reflection and choice, or whether they are forever destined to depend . . . on accident and force."

Government by reflection and choice called for a new style of leadership and a new quality of followership. It required leaders to be responsive to popular concerns, and it required followers to be active and informed participants in the process. Democracy does not eliminate emotion from politics; sometimes it fosters demagoguery; but it is confident that, as the greatest of democratic leaders put it, you cannot fool all of the people all of the time. It measures leadership by results and retires those who overreach or falter or fail.

It is true that in the long run despots are measured by results too. But they can postpone the day of judgment, sometimes indefinitely, and in the meantime they can do infinite harm. It is also true that democracy is no guarantee of virtue and intelligence in government, for the voice of the people is not necessarily the voice of God. But democracy, by assuring the right of opposition, offers built-in resistance to the evils inherent in absolutism. As the theologian Reinhold Niebuhr summed it up, "Man's capacity for justice makes democracy possible, but man's inclination to injustice makes democracy necessary."

A second test for leadership is the end for which power is sought. When leaders have as their goal the supremacy of a master race or the promotion of totalitarian revolution or the acquisition and exploitation of colonies or the protection of greed and privilege or the preservation of personal power, it is likely that their leadership will do little to advance the cause of humanity. When their goal is the abolition of slavery, the liberation of women, the enlargement of opportunity for the poor and powerless, the extension of equal rights to racial minorities, the defense of the freedoms of expression and opposition, it is likely that their leadership will increase the sum of human liberty and welfare.

Leaders have done great harm to the world. They have also conferred great benefits. You will find both sorts in this series. Even "good" leaders must be regarded with a certain wariness. Leaders are not demigods; they put on their trousers one leg after another just like ordinary mortals. No leader is infallible, and every leader needs to be reminded of this at regular intervals. Irreverence irritates leaders but is their salvation. Unquestioning submission corrupts leaders and demeans followers. Making a cult of a leader is always a mistake. Fortunately hero worship generates its own antidote. "Every hero," said Emerson, "becomes a bore at last."

The signal benefit the great leaders confer is to embolden the rest of us to live according to our own best selves, to be active, insistent, and resolute in affirming our own sense of things. For great leaders attest to the reality of human freedom against the supposed inevitabilities of history. And they attest to the wisdom and power that may lie within the most unlikely of us, which is why Abraham Lincoln remains the supreme example of great leadership. A great leader, said Emerson, exhibits new possibilities to all humanity. "We feed on genius. . . . Great men exist that there may be greater men."

Great leaders, in short, justify themselves by emancipating and empowering their followers. So humanity struggles to master its destiny, remembering with Alexis de Tocqueville: "It is true that around every man a fatal circle is traced beyond which he cannot pass; but within the wide verge of that circle he is powerful and free; as it is with man, so with communities."

1

Son of the Desert

Qaddafi's puritanism . . . went back to his Bedouin origins.
—JOHN K. COOLEY
American journalist

Those who were boys then are men now. Still, they remember their quiet but intense classmate, the strange, thin boy from the desert whose face had been pockmarked by sandstorms and toughened by the strong Sahara sun, and whose soft, dark eyes could focus suddenly with a sharp urgency. They remember that even in those days Muammar el-Qaddafi was not like the rest of them, that he was somehow special.

Qaddafi was considered unusual in part because he had had a very different upbringing than most of the boys at the Islamic grammar school in Sirte, Libya. During the 1950s, Libya's 1 million inhabitants were divided into two distinct groups — those who lived in modern cities located along the thin strip of mild Mediterranean coastline and those who roamed the Sahara Desert, the vast, arid wasteland that makes up most of the country's territory. The majority of Qaddafi's classmates belonged to the former category, hailing from cities like Tripoli, Benghazi, Tobruk, and Sirte itself. They were sons of merchants, businessmen, or high-ranking military officers.

Born into a tribe of desert nomads in 1942, Muammar el-Qaddafi rose meteorically to become leader of Libya at the age of 27. In attempting to transform a small nation into a world power, the mercurial Qaddafi would adopt an interventionist foreign policy that would confound and consternate his fellow world leaders.

AP/WIDE WORLD PHOTOS

By contrast, Qaddafi was born in 1942 into a family of nomadic tribesmen, or Bedouins, who lived amid the drifting sands of that part of the Sahara known as the Sirtic Desert and eked out a bare existence raising small herds of cattle or sheep. Residing in temporary shelters made out of goatskin and wooden poles, they had no electricity or running water. His father, Abu Meniar el-Qaddafi, and his mother, Aissha el-Qaddafi, were Berbers, a Libyan ethnic minority descended from the herdsmen who inhabited North Africa prior to the Arab invasions of the 7th century. They belonged to the Qaddafa tribe, whose members lived in the same communal manner their ancestors had adopted many centuries earlier — sharing living quarters and work responsibilities.

UPI/BETTMANN NEWSPHOTOS

A Tuareg tribesman plays a traditional tune on a bagpipe fashioned from animal skins. The Tuareg are one of the many nomadic tribes that roam the desert sands of the inhospitable Sahara, living in primitive tents and raising small herds of goats and sheep. Qaddafi was raised in this way of life as a member of a Berber tribe.

In the Qaddafi family, religion played a much larger role than it did in the families of many of Muammar's classmates at the Sirte school. Daily life in the Qaddafa clan revolved around the beliefs and rituals of the Islamic religion. The youngest of the world's major religions, Islam is based on the teachings of the 6th- and 7th-century prophet Muhammad — as recorded in the Muslim holy book, the Koran — and considers itself to be the fulfillment of the older faiths of Christianity and Judaism. Like most Libyans, the Qaddafa tribe belonged to the Sunni, or orthodox, branch of Islam (to which 90 percent of the world's Muslims adhere). Sunnism is distinguished from the major dissident branch, the Shi'ite sect, by a different conception of who Muhammad's spiritual heirs were and by its followers' acceptance of the *Sunna*, the body of Muhammad's sayings and customs that is used to supplement the Koran. At an early age, Qaddafi learned to perform the daily ritual of the orthodox Muslim. Five times a day he would wash himself, fall to his knees facing in the direction of the Muslim holy city of Mecca, and pray to God, or Allah as he is known in Arabic.

Qaddafi had also been imbued during his early years with an intense hatred of Europeans, unlike his urban classmates, many of whose fathers fraternized regularly with Libya's many foreign businessmen. The Qaddafi family's xenophobia (fear or hatred of foreigners) derived from Libya's long history of foreign domination. At the time of Qaddafi's birth, the sovereign nation of Libya did not yet exist. It had been an Italian colony since 1911 and before that a loose collection of provinces belonging to a series of conquering empires. Prior to the 20th century, the history of Libya is in fact the history of tribes, cities, and the three main regions — Tripolitania, Cyrenaica, and the Fezzan. In antiquity, portions of Cyrenaica, the eastern province of Libya, were colonized by the Greeks and the Romans, while parts of Tripolitania, the northwestern province centered around the bustling seaport of Tripoli, were ruled by Phoenicia and then Carthage. Later, from 642 to 663, all three regions were invaded and conquered by the Arabs, who by the 11th century had converted the population to Islam. From the 16th century until the Italian colonization, the area was dominated by the Ottoman Empire. For much of its history the unification of Libya proved difficult because of the area's geography: the western provinces of Fezzan and Tripolitania are separated from Cyrenaica by the Sirtic Desert, which begins at the Gulf of Sidra and extends hundreds of miles inland.

In the early 1900s, Italy, which had watched France and Great Britain gain colonial dominion over much of Africa, decided to acquire its own stake in the area. Setting its sights on the region that is now Libya, Italy launched a war of conquest against the Turks in 1911. Several of Qaddafi's relatives fought the Italians in the local Libyan resistance movement led by the legendary Omar al-Mokhtar. Qaddafi's grandfather was killed in the fighting and his father and uncle served long sentences in Italian jails after being taken as prisoners of war. As a child, Qaddafi heard countless stories about the atrocities committed by the Italian armies. It was said that captured Libyans had been dropped alive from Italian airplanes and that thousands of desert dwellers had died when the Italians covered their precious wells with cement and slaughtered their herds. In 1932 Italy finally wrested control of the inland area

UPI/BETTMANN NEWSPHOTOS

A Berber farmer inspects a network of caves used to store agricultural products. The Berbers are descended from the original, pre-Arab inhabitants of North Africa. As leader of Libya, Qaddafi would seek to limit the power of the desert tribes and their chieftains.

from the fierce guerrilla fighters.

In Qaddafi's first year, his homeland became the focus of the struggle between the Allied forces of Great Britain, France, and the United States and the Axis powers of Germany and Italy for control of North Africa. Libyans saw the war as a golden opportunity to push for independence from Italy and organized military forces, led by Muhammed Idris al-Sanusi, to support the Allies. The campaign swept back and forth three times over the Libyan desert. A famous battle took place in the port city of Tobruk. Led by the "Desert Fox," Erwin Rommel, the Germans captured Tobruk in June 1942. Supported by the *Sanusis* — volunteer forces from the charismatic Islamic religious order led by Idris — the British repeatedly attempted to retake the city. Ultimately, they were successful, and by 1943 the Allies had liberated all of Libya. British military governments assumed leadership in Tripolitania and Cyrenaica and France administered the Fezzan. After the war, Italy renounced all claims to the territory. By a treaty in February 1947, it was established that Great Britain, France, the United States, and the Soviet Union would determine Libya's future status. The Big Powers bickered interminably over the question because of Libya's tremendous strategic importance as a location from which to control Mediterranean sea lanes. Finally, the question was given to the United Nations, which decided in 1949 that Libya should become an independent state. In 1951 a national assembly composed of an equal number of representatives from Libya's three regions drafted the independence constitution. On December 24, 1951, Muhammed Idris al-Sanusi became King Idris I and formally declared Libya to be independent.

When the 10-year-old Muammar el-Qaddafi arrived at the Islamic school in Sirte, his upbringing was not the only thing that set apart this son of the desert. He was also remarkably intelligent. This was why his family was willing to spend its meager savings on an expensive boarding-school education. "My son is possessed of an unusual intelligence. To educate him will bring blessings from Allah," his father had said. At Sirte, he easily shot to the top of his class and skipped a number of grade levels.

From the beginning of Qaddafi's stay at Sirte, his classmates also noticed his obsession with the transistor radio his parents had bought for him. At the outset, he listened merely to relieve his boredom and allay his fears about being in a new environment. Sometimes he would scrimp on food so he could afford to buy new batteries. He always seemed to be listening.

Eventually, the radio helped to create in Qaddafi the trait that truly made him different: a sense of political awareness. At the age of 12 or 13, Qaddafi began to listen exclusively to the "Voice of the Arabs" programs transmitted from Cairo, Egypt. These broadcasts featured speeches by Egyptian President Gamal Abdel Nasser. Nasser was an energetic, charismatic leader who had taken the Arab world by storm after leading the Free Officers' Movement, a group of young Egyptian military officers, in a successful coup d'état against King Farouk in 1952. Nasser had become premier in 1954, and he had carried out much-needed political and economic reforms, redistributing the large estates of corrupt landowners and abolishing the deposed monarchy's practice of taking bribes and playing favorites with

AP/WIDE WORLD PHOTOS

Part of an Italian parachuting unit, Libyans stand at attention during World War II. Many of their countrymen, including Libya's future king, Idris, fought for the British and American forces. In 1943, a year after Qaddafi's birth, the Allies gained control of North Africa, ending 32 years of Italian colonial rule in Libya.

> ***Raise your head, my brother in North Africa. The sun of freedom is rising over Egypt and the whole of the Nile Valley will soon be flooded by its rays. Raise your heads to the skies.***
>
> —from a "Voice of the Arabs" broadcast

the rich. He had encouraged a growing sense of Egyptian nationalism by reducing foreign economic influence in his nation and maintaining neutrality in the Cold War between the United States and the Soviet Union. Above all, he had become the standard-bearer for the Pan-Arab movement, a movement that sought to extend political cooperation among the many Middle Eastern states with Arabic-speaking populations (including Libya, Egypt, Tunisia, Morocco, Syria, Lebanon, Iraq, Jordan, Saudi Arabia, and Yemen).

The Arab unity movement had grown out of widespread resentment in the Arab world of its recent domination by European powers. After World War I, when the Ottoman Empire's defeat seemed to promise freedom for its Arab provinces, the newly established League of Nations had divided up much of the Middle East between France and Great Britain. In 1945, after several Arab states had managed to gain their independence, they formed an alliance called the Arab League to express their resentment of imperialism and to oppose the attempt to establish a Jewish state in Palestine. Their efforts in regard to the latter goal proved futile when, in 1947, Great Britain, the colonial ruler of Palestine, asked the United Nations to determine the area's future status. Amid growing tension between Arabs and Jews — who had been immigrating to Palestine in large numbers since Britain's receipt of a mandate in 1922 — the UN divided Palestine into separate Jewish and Arab states. When the nation of Israel was officially declared in 1948, the Arab League immediately attacked, sparking a two-year war, the first of five Arab-Israeli conflicts.

In his highly charged radio addresses, Nasser called for Arab nations to reject their tradition of fraternal rivalry and conflict and join together around two collective interests: the practice of their common religion, Islam, and the defeat of their common enemy, Israel. The establishment of Israel, according to Nasser, had violated the territorial claims of Arabs living there (known as Palestinians) and represented an attempt by what he called "selfish imperialist nations" to reap material and strategic

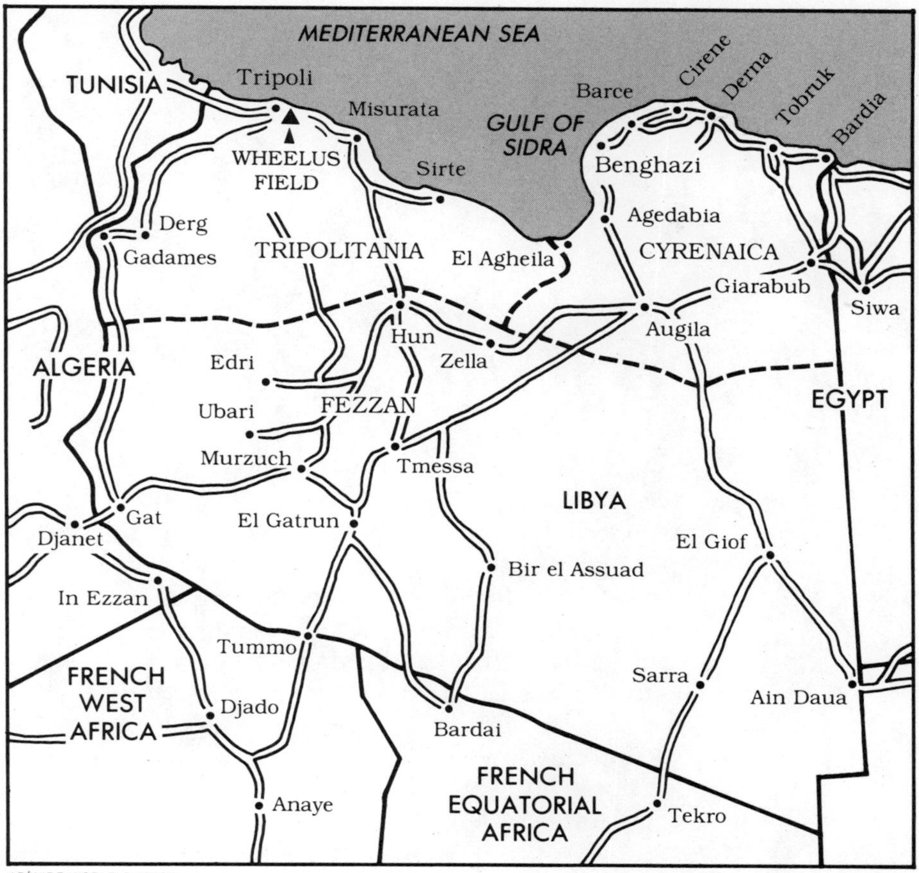

AP/WIDE WORLD PHOTOS

The borders of Libya as of December 24, 1951, when, under the auspices of the United Nations, the country achieved its independence. Located in North Africa along the Mediterranean Sea, Libya is one-fifth the size of the United States and is divided into three regions: Tripolitania, Cyrenaica, and the Fezzan.

rewards under the guise of an ostensibly altruistic purpose: to provide a homeland for the Jews. Nasser's ultimate goal was to establish a unified state composed of all Arab nations. The first step toward such an Arab nation would be for each separate Arab country to develop a fierce nationalism of its own. Moreover, Nasser maintained, it was the duty of every Arab to guarantee that his or her country supported and actively pursued each of these Pan-Arab goals.

Nasser's message appealed to Qaddafi for a number of reasons. First of all, the Egyptian leader had articulated Qaddafi's dislike of Europeans. In addition, Nasser was an engaging, forceful speaker who made one believe his promises to return the

When Qaddafi was 10 years old, his parents sent him to an Islamic boys' school much like this American-built facility in Tripoli. As a boarding student in Sirte, Qaddafi quickly shot to the top of his class and began to develop an interest in political affairs.

UPI/BETTMANN NEWSPHOTOS

Arab world to the glory it had not experienced since the 11th century, when, as a powerful empire, it boasted the world's richest culture and intellectual life. Moreover, coming from a conservative, impoverished background, Qaddafi appreciated Nasser's commitment to Islam and to improving the health and welfare of Egypt's poor.

From the time he heard these broadcasts, Qaddafi dedicated himself to bringing Nasserism to Libya. As a young student, he quickly determined that Libya's King Idris I was too friendly with western imperialist nations, especially with Israel's close allies, Great Britain and the United States. The king also had unfairly hoarded what little wealth the nation had for himself. Furthermore, Idris was guilty of not actively seeking Arab unity and not incorporating the Islamic religion into his government. Though barely a teenager, Qaddafi vowed someday to replace the Libyan monarchy with Nasser's unique fusion of egalitarian economic principles and aggressively independent conduct of foreign affairs.

In idle moments, Qaddafi dreamed of "leading his people out of poverty." Many of his classmates at the Sirte school were amused by his precocious political commitment. "If you like Nasser so much, Muammar, you should become an Egyptian," they teased him. He would not answer. He only became more convinced that he was on the right path.

Graduating from Sirte with honors, Qaddafi went to the city of Sebha to attend secondary school. There, shortly after his 14th birthday, he began in earnest to make plans for his revolution against King Idris. The school at Sebha was not as exclusive as the one at Sirte had been. The student body included several sons of poor families, boys from the desert, like Qaddafi. These boys were easily recruited as allies in Qaddafi's revolutionary schemes.

From the outset, Qaddafi was their unquestioned leader. His decisiveness and his sense of purpose made him the kind of boy whom others follow. He had charisma. In 1956 he and three other Sebha students formed their first revolutionary cell, or group, with the long-range goal of overthrowing the

Qaddafi took to the gospel of revolution at an early age, modeling himself at various times on Egypt's Gamal Abdel Nasser and China's Mao Tse-tung, among others.
—*Newsweek* magazine

UPI/BETTMANN NEWSPHOTOS

Libya's first leader, King Idris I (left), meets with President Gamal Abdel Nasser of Egypt in June 1956. Later that year, Nasser would nationalize the Suez Canal, securing his position as the dominant figure in the Arab world. Qaddafi, then in high school, was captivated by Nasser's calls for Arab unity.

He told all of his schoolmates to prepare for a military career, since that was the only way to make a revolution.

—JOHN K. COOLEY
American journalist, on Qaddafi's student years

king and the more immediate goal of stirring up, through demonstrations, popular support for Nasser's Pan-Arab program. Qaddafi also decided that members of the cell should take classes at Sebha that would prepare them for military careers. In the army, he reasoned, the young conspirators would have the best opportunity to change Libyan society and be in an advantageous position from which to stage a coup d'état.

Qaddafi conceived the system by which these cells would grow. Each of the four boys would form a new and separate cell—called a "second cell"—consisting of himself and three other boys. Each of the boys in these new cells would in turn go out and form yet another cell of four boys, and so on. Under Qaddafi's careful direction, these cells were kept separate from one another. Each boy knew only about the activities of two cells — the one he had originally joined and the one he had himself formed. In this way, Qaddafi limited the amount of information a young conspirator could reveal if captured and tortured by King Idris's secret police.

Only Qaddafi knew all of the members of his organization. He was the sole member who had the

UPI/BETTMANN NEWSPHOTOS

King Farouk of Egypt waits for service in a small restaurant in Nice, France, shortly after being deposed. To the young Qaddafi, the inequitable policies of King Idris I were reminiscent of the former Egyptian ruler's corrupt regime.

UPI/BETTMANN NEWSPHOTOS

A Libyan belly dancer gyrates before American servicemen at a café in Tripoli. Raised a devout follower of Islam — a religion that condemns alcohol, gambling, and premarital sex — Qaddafi was disgusted by the proliferation of nightclubs that followed King Idris's welcoming of Western military bases in the 1950s.

power to reject applicants. That he himself would betray his followers under torture never concerned Qaddafi. He knew that he would die first, and the other boys all trusted him as much as he trusted himself.

When Qaddafi organized and led pro-Nasser and anti-Israeli marches, the police decided that he constituted a threat to the monarchy. They began to monitor his movements, hoping to intimidate him. Some of the students at Sebha who supported the king issued threats to Qaddafi. In the end, the police decided that his radical activities could no longer be tolerated. They went to the Sebha school authorities. Qaddafi was expelled from school for "treasonable behavior."

But the son of the desert was not concerned. He had his Muslim faith. He had his purpose.

WELCOME TO TRIPOLI

2

September Coup

> ***With one blow from your heroic army, the idols collapsed and the graven images shattered.***
> —MUAMMAR EL-QADDAFI announcing to the Libyans the overthrow of King Idris

During Qaddafi's early years, Libya was one of the poorest countries in the world — mostly a consequence of its unfortunate topography. Ninety-five percent of the country is desert. Only 2 percent of the land is arable. The country has no permanent rivers and receives rain about once every three years. But, in 1959, when Qaddafi was a high school student, Libya discovered a natural resource that would change its fortunes for years to come: oil. King Idris's government made a huge profit auctioning off drilling rights to, and imposing stiff taxes on, a spate of foreign oil companies. Libya's oil was considered a hot commodity because it was cheaply made into gasoline as a result of its low sulfur content. Ultimately, the country's proximity to Europe would enable it to become one of the world's major oil exporters. By the 1980s, oil revenues would soar to $23.2 billion. But under King Idris, little of the new wealth was passed on to the common people. This only stiffened Qaddafi's resolve to bring about revolution.

Qaddafi finished his high school education at the Misurata school, where he established a new net-

British troops on maneuvers in Tripoli in 1958. Under King Idris I, Libya entered into treaties with both Great Britain and the United States and received generous economic aid in return. Domestic resentment of this policy first surfaced in 1956, when the Arab-Israeli War prompted fierce nationalist riots.

AP/WIDE WORLD PHOTOS

Before 1969 Libya was one of the poorest countries in the Third World. The Mercedeses and Cadillacs of the elite few who were made wealthy by oil raced through Tripoli and Benghazi streets ignoring the donkey carts, burden-laden camels, and shacks of the overwhelming number of people who lived at bare subsistence level.

—JOHN K. COOLEY
American journalist

work of revolutionary cells. To keep track of the members and communicate with the leaders of the cells, Qaddafi made up a secret code. He knew that police spies were still watching him, but he tricked them into thinking that he was participating only in anti-Israeli activities and Nasser "discussion groups." Actually, at the age of 17, he was building a remarkably broad insurgent network.

Members of Qaddafi's revolutionary cells had watched with dismay during the 1950s as King Idris extended Libya's cooperation with the West. Libya signed a 20-year defense treaty with Great Britain in 1953 and soon thereafter agreed to a similar pact with the United States, which, among other items, called for Libya to receive $40 million in American economic aid. Idris also accepted without reservations the presence of three foreign military installations — two British bases, at Tobruk and El Adem, and the United States' Wheelus Air Force Base, outside of Tripoli. Wheelus had been hastily set up by the United States in 1950 during the Korean War, and after Idris came to power, it was put to a succession of uses — as a training base for the North Atlantic Treaty Organization (NATO), as a link in the Strategic Air Command (the air-based portion of the U.S. nuclear defense system) and as the headquarters of the U.S. 17th Air Force. In an effort to offset the anti-imperialist broadcasts of Cairo's "Voice of the Arabs," the United States also built a powerful radio station in Benghazi to broadcast pro-Western propaganda. By 1959 the U.S. aid mission in Libya had become one of the largest in the world, with advisers and technicians operating in all sectors of the national and regional governments. Libya's extensive contacts with the West infuriated Qaddafi and his cohorts, who thought that their nation's political independence was being undermined and its cultural integrity threatened.

The young conspirators were also disconcerted by political repression under Idris. According to the constitution instituted at the time of Libya's independence, the country was supposed to be governed by a tripartite system featuring a house of

UPI/BETTMANN NEWSPHOTOS

Idris I at the time of his assumption of power in December 1951. Though his government was ostensibly a constitutional monarchy based on the British system, Idris suppressed political parties and filled the Libyan parliament with handpicked supporters.

representatives, a senate, and the king himself — all of whom could enact laws. But the king, following a hard-fought, at times violent, political campaign in 1952, had quickly subverted this democratic structure by outlawing all political parties. In suppressing political parties, Idris forced the opposition underground, leaving groups like Qaddafi's that objected to the ruler's policies with only one alternative —to work clandestinely for the king's overthrow.

Qaddafi graduated with honors from Misurata and entered the University of Libya, where he studied history and political science and continued to plot the overthrow of the king. He also held secret meetings to discuss plans for the political system his revolution would install in place of King Idris's government. He proposed to his followers that the legal code in the new state should incorporate the *Sharia* — the Muslim sacred law. He also followed Nasser's lead in proposing that Libya adopt certain elements of socialism. In 1962 Nasser had outlined his program for political, economic, and social development and called it "Arab socialism." Unlike Soviet communism, Nasser's plan allowed for the

This ramshackle dwelling housed an entire Libyan family in the 1950s. During its first years of independence, Libya was a poor nation, with an estimated per capita income of $40. As a young student, Qaddafi envisioned a Libya in which wealth would be redistributed to the working class and the poor.

UPI/BETTMANN NEWSPHOTOS

practice of religion and rejected the idea that the state should be run by a dictatorship of the proletariat, or working classes. It did, however, accept socialist principles in envisioning communal ownership of some types of property, government operation of industry, state distribution of health care, and, in general, the creation of a large public sector of the economy. Above all, it applauded the socialist notion that it was the state's responsibility to implement social justice by improving the welfare of the poor and working classes through the redistribution of wealth and the enhancement of their political power.

Qaddafi was careful to distinguish what he himself called "Bedouin socialism" from the Marxist-Leninist philosophy of the Soviet Union. In college, while studying political science, he had come to view capitalism — the free-market economic system adopted by most Western democracies — and Soviet communism as twin evils. He was especially concerned that the two superpowers, the Soviet Union and the United States, would try to exploit Libya's newfound oil wealth.

Qaddafi was 21 years old in 1963 when he graduated from the University of Libya with a law diploma. He did not choose to pursue a career in law, but instead enrolled in the Libyan Military College in Benghazi, where he resumed his revolutionary organizing. Again Qaddafi sought out classmates from poor families and desert backgrounds. The academy's proximity to the University of Benghazi enabled Qaddafi to initiate contacts with other dissidents and to expand his network. It was around this time that he dubbed his first and second cells the Secret Unionist Free Officers' Movement in emulation of Nasser's military conspiracy against King Farouk. His movement proved especially attractive to devoutly religious students, who appreciated Qaddafi's devotion to Islam and his insistence that his followers observe "revolutionary disciplines."

In one terrible moment of fate, the darkness of ages —from the rule of the Turks to the tyranny of the Italians and the era of reaction, bribery, intercession, favoritism, treason and treachery — was dispersed. From now on, Libya is deemed a free, sovereign republic under the name of the Libyan Arab Republic, ascending with God's help to exalted heights.

—MUAMMAR EL-QADDAFI
announcing the overthrow
of King Idris

Thus, Qaddafi's recruits differed from the other cadets at Benghazi not only in their radical political beliefs but in their adoption of the ascetic lifestyle called for by Islam. Most of the young soldiers-to-be spent their evenings in raucous revelry. They smoked, drank, gambled, frequented cabarets, flirted with young women, and even spent time in brothels. In contrast, Qaddafi and his compatriots followed the strict rules of the Koran, which forbids the use of alcohol and tobacco, prohibits gambling, and condemns premarital sex. Their puritanism was, according to American writer John K. Cooley, "in part a reaction against the creeping corruption spread by the foreign oil companies and contractors that jockeyed for positions and favors under [King Idris's] regime."

In 1965 Qaddafi graduated at the top of his class and received a commission as a lieutenant in the Libyan army. He was quickly dispatched for advanced training to Beaconsfield, England, where he studied British signal corps tactics. This training in communications would later help him in coordinating various branches of his organizations.

Back in Libya after nine months, he began positioning his men within the army to act most effectively when it was time to make the move against King Idris. In August 1969 Qaddafi was made a captain in the Libyan army's signal corps.

During this time, Qaddafi had been quietly gathering information on the king's secret police. He learned that the organization was riddled with corruption and inefficiency and that Libya's security forces, including the king's personal bodyguard, were careless and given to heavy drinking. Quietly, Qaddafi's officers now began recruiting the rank-and-file soldiers to their cause. The time to stage the coup was at hand.

But before they could act, something strange happened. An older officer, who was not a member of Qaddafi's secret society, approached him and tried to enlist him in a separate scheme to overthrow the government. Qaddafi was taken aback. After all the years of planning, he had no interest in participating in someone else's revolution. He stalled the older man by saying he needed more time to think the offer over.

But Qaddafi would not join the other group, or combine forces with it, because in his view they lacked the purity of purpose that had been guiding him for over 12 years. Instead, he decided to move quickly lest the older plotters steal his carefully planned revolution from him. In the early morning hours of September 1, 1969, while King Idris was vacationing in Turkey, Qaddafi acted.

Tell President Nasser we made this revolution for him. He can take everything of ours and add it to the rest of the Arab world's resources to be used for battle.

—MUAMMAR EL-QADDAFI
after ousting King Idris

The coup was brilliantly conceived and deftly executed. It was begun by a group of army officers who led several platoons of soldiers through Tripoli and seized control of the king's palace. They employed an ingenious tactic: the previous day, conspirators belonging to three armored-car battalions had received permission for a night training exercise. Instead of conducting the exercise, they drove into Tripoli and disarmed the Tripoli police. Simultaneously, Lieutenant Colonel Musa Ahmed led a small team of soldiers, armed with handguns and driving Volkswagens, in an assault on Gurnada, a desert military camp that housed Idris's first line of defense, the Cyrenaica Defense Force (CYDEF). With the help of sympathizers from the CYDEF, the team quickly subdued the camp, though sporadic gunfire killed one and left fifteen wounded. In other Libyan cities, several hundred military officers loyal to Qaddafi took police officers and other key members of the old regime into custody. Qaddafi himself rode at the head of a column of tanks through Benghazi and seized the radio station — the same station that the United States had financed a decade earlier.

Qaddafi issued an anonymous broadcast announcing the coup, telling the Libyan people that in the name of Allah, his group had overthrown the "reactionary, backward, and decadent regime" of King Idris and replaced it with a Libyan Arab Republic. The speech called for the Libyans to "stand together against the enemy of the Arab nation, the enemy of Islam, the enemy of humanity who destroyed our holy places and shattered our honor" — Israel. The impassioned speech promised that the new rulers would attempt to restore the glory lost to centuries of foreign rule. Its final words brought Libya into a new era: "O you who witnessed the holy

UPI/BETTMANN NEWSPHOTOS

A worker lays cable in the Libyan desert in preparation for oil-drilling tests. After the first major oil discovery in 1959, Libya, unlike Middle Eastern states that granted a single oil concession, sold drilling rights to several foreign companies. Libya's low-sulfur crude was prized for its easy convertibility to gasoline.

war, who fought the good fight . . . O sons of the steppes, sons of the ancient cities, the upright countryside, O sons of the villages . . . the hour of work has come. Forward."

Foreign countries were at first confused about how to react to the coup. No government had had any previous contact with the young conspirators, and not even Egypt had any information on their political orientation. Qaddafi did not help matters by remaining anonymous during the first days of the revolution. In Turkey, King Idris reportedly told an aide that the coup was a "trifling affair," fully expecting that the United States and Great Britain would help restore his regime. Secret clauses of a 1953 Anglo-Libyan treaty stipulated that the British were obligated to intervene militarily in the event the Libyan monarchy was threatened. But Britain refused to honor the treaty, afraid of alienating other Arab nations and worried about suspicious Soviet naval movements in the Mediterranean. By September 5, Idris had passed his claim to the throne to his son Crown Prince Hassan al-Reda, who, after being arrested, renounced his claim and

Arab orphans enjoy toys sent by an American women's club in 1955. King Idris's close relationship with the West brought economic benefits, but Qaddafi opposed such ties, feeling that the country's traditional way of life was endangered by the influx of Western advisers.

UPI/BETTMANN NEWSPHOTOS

UPI/BETTMANN NEWSPHOTOS

Led by Qaddafi's second-in-command, Abdel Salem Jalloud, Libyan army officers captured the state palace in Tripoli in a dawn attack on September 1, 1969. On the same morning Qaddafi, who was a communications specialist in the army, seized a radio station in Benghazi and broadcast news of the coup. Idris was vacationing in Turkey at the time.

urged the Libyan people to support the new regime.

At the time of the coup, Arab leaders were gathered for a summit conference in Cairo. Arab monarchs like King Hassan II of Morocco and King Faisal of Saudi Arabia were disturbed by the news of another king's dethroning. Nasser was confused — he had expected a coup but from another quarter, from supporters of the crown prince. Qaddafi and his men conveyed word to the Egyptian Embassy in Tripoli that they wanted to meet with an Egyptian envoy, preferably Nasser himself. Instead, Muhammad Haykal, editor of an Egyptian newspaper, traveled from Cairo. Upon meeting Haykal, Qaddafi told him, "We do not want to rule Libya. All we have done is our duty as nationalists. Now it is for President Nasser to take over himself and guide Libya from the reactionary camp, where it was, to the progressive camp, where it should be." Haykal reported back to Nasser that Qaddafi was "shockingly innocent" and "scandalously pure."

The young military officers who staged the coup proclaimed a Socialist Libyan Arab Republic, suspended the constitution, and dissolved the king's parliament. The military junta established as the new governing body a 12-man Revolutionary Command Council (RCC). Qaddafi became a colonel in

AP/WIDE WORLD PHOTOS

The day after the September coup, these Libyan students took over their nation's embassy in Damascus, Syria, and removed the portrait of the deposed king. The Arab nationalist message of Libya's new rulers — who were all in their twenties — gained them widespread support among Libyan youth.

the army and was named chairman of the council, becoming, at age 27, the de facto leader of Libya. A provisional constitution that would be installed in December would proclaim Libya "an Arab democratic and free republic which constitutes a part of the Arab nation and whose objective is comprehensive Arab unity."

You can't imagine how pure he is.
—MUSTAFA AL-KHAROUBI
participant in Qaddafi's coup to oust Idris, on Qaddafi

Once in power, Qaddafi was determined that even the poorest Bedouin farmer would benefit from Libya's oil wealth. But even though the RCC took measures to gain more control over the oil industry than Idris had exercised, not as much money was available to spread around as Qaddafi would have liked. Although in 1972 the RCC would implement a three-year, $6-million development plan, social and economic planning occurred in a haphazard, trial-and-error fashion for the first two years after the revolution. The RCC had greater success in pursuing another goal: consolidating its power by weakening the old Libyan elite. To begin with, most of the high-ranking army officers were arrested. A "people's court" was convened to investigate each member of the old regime in order to determine whether he had made his money through bribes or other corrupt methods, in which case he was sent to jail. Most Italian settlers were expelled from the country and their substantial holdings were confiscated and divided up among Libya's lower classes. The RCC also sought to do away with tribal chieftains, who had been immensely powerful under Idris. Political hierarchies within the tribes were dismantled and traditional tribal boundaries were no longer considered to be valid geographical divisions.

As a prelude to Libya's later incorporation of Islamic law into its constitution, Qaddafi began to enforce the Muslim prohibition against alcohol. To do so, he started a personal campaign to close the nightclubs that had proliferated during Idris's reign. To Qaddafi's mind, the new Libya was supposed to be a serious land dedicated to the task of building a larger Arab nation. The frivolity of nightclubs did not belong.

One night, dressed in his army uniform, Qaddafi led a platoon of military police into a nightclub called the Bowdlerina. It was a lavish place where rich merchants and foreign businessmen went to have fun. As Qaddafi entered, the floor show was in progress — 16 young women dancing in revealing costumes. He climbed onto the stage and pulled his gun from its holster. The audience, thinking he was one of the performers, applauded generously. Then Qaddafi fired his gun at the ceiling three times. The members of the chorus ran, terrified, for the wings. The customers dived under the tables. "This evil place is officially closed as of now!" Qaddafi announced. "It will not reopen," he added. To guarantee his order, the military police began to pull down the plush draperies and attack the gilded woodwork with axes.

Such dramatic acts endeared Qaddafi to the Bedouins and the urban poor, but not always to the rest of Libya's citizens. Many of the wealthier and better-educated Libyans disapproved of their new leader's laws and of his flamboyant enforcement of them. Two who felt this way were Colonel Adam Hawaz and Colonel Musa Ahmed, respectively, the minister of defense and the minister of the interior in the new administration Qaddafi had set up. Both officers had been prominent in the old regime but had been included in Qaddafi's coup because of their foreign connections. After the September takeover they had been assigned to explain the coup to American and British diplomatic personnel and to assure foreign oil companies that the coup would not interrupt prior drilling arrangements.

The two colonels did not agree with Qaddafi's strict regulation of personal behavior. They thought that questions of morality like drinking, smoking, and dancing should be the domain of religious authorities, not the government. Also, they were wary of Qaddafi's unmitigated devotion to President Nasser of Egypt, fearing that Qaddafi might make Libya a mere satellite to Egypt. They decided to act on their fears before Qaddafi became more firmly entrenched. They plotted a countercoup to take place

AP/WIDE WORLD PHOTOS

Qaddafi pictured shortly after taking power. In a radio proclamation during the coup, he stated that his men had been sent by Allah to destroy "the reactionary, backward, and decadent" regime of Idris I. His address also revealed what would be the major goals of his government: to destroy Israel, to build Arab unity, and to establish a socialist republic based on Islamic law.

in mid-December of 1969, a little more than three months after King Idris had been deposed.

It would be the first of many unsuccessful attempts to end Qaddafi's rule over Libya. Like many

When they began to learn from the sufferings of the 1967 setbacks by Israel, it was the overpowering conditions prevailing in Libya which fashioned and polished the core of their revolutionary characters. From suppression they derived an urge to spring forward; from observing corruption they gained ideals; and from their isolation they learned the importance of unity.

—MUHAMMAD HAYKAL
editor of an Egyptian newspaper, on Qaddafi and his supporters

of those that would follow, it sought logistical and financial aid from foreign sources. Colonels Hawaz and Ahmed tried to convince British and American diplomats to back their scheme. But Great Britain and the United States had welcomed the replacement of King Idris, even though they had installed his government in the first place. They had become suspicious of Idris after the discovery of oil, when he had insisted on a reduced Western military presence and fewer economic ties. They also wanted more time to determine whether Qaddafi would prove a sympathetic business partner — whether he would be willing to sell Libyan oil at attractive prices — and so were very upset when they learned of plans for a countercoup.

Indeed, they were so upset that they leaked news of the scheme to Qaddafi. He arrested the two ministers and six fellow conspirators. All went to prison. Over the next few years, the United States would continue to provide significant support and even Central Intelligence Agency (CIA) protection for the Qaddafi regime, in spite of his hostile remarks about imperialism, his aggressive oil policies, and his eventual closure of Western military bases. More important from the American standpoint was that Qaddafi spoke out against communism and funded other anticommunist governments.

During those few months immediately following his rise to power, Qaddafi was much occupied with two other matters. One was establishing relations with and earning the respect of other Arab rulers, particularly Egypt's President Nasser. The other was his rapid-fire courtship of Fathia Nouri Kahled. She was a former schoolteacher and the daughter of a Libyan army officer. Their wedding took place on December 25, 1969. It was a romantic midnight ceremony at which Qaddafi's loyal fundamentalist officers formed an arch with crossed swords for the exit of the bride and groom.

And to sweeten the moment, indeed, to make it complete, Qaddafi's boyhood idol, President Gamal Abdel Nasser of Egypt, was at his side during the Muslim ritual.

UPI/BETTMANN NEWSPHOTOS

Qaddafi entertains foreign journalists in his Bedouin tent at the Bab al-Azzizia barracks in Tripoli. In 1969 Libya's new government, the Revolutionary Command Council (RCC), established its headquarters at this military base. After the coup, foreign governments scrambled to find information on Libya's new leaders — who were unknown even to their hero, Nasser.

3

Arab Republic

Internally, its people have become prosperous, and seem to lack nothing materially. Externally, Libya is flanked by fearful or jealous neighbors, and has few real friends.
—JOHN K. COOLEY
American journalist

As it happened, neither his marriage nor his ambition to be an important Arab leader worked out well for Qaddafi. His wife Fathia became pregnant but their love did not flourish. And, although from the beginning Nasser had taken Qaddafi under his wing, the young Libyan had a difficult time establishing friendly relations with the rest of the heads of the Arab world.

He first encountered Arab leaders at an Arab summit conference in Rabat, Morocco, in January 1970. He immediately alienated his fellow statesmen by aggressively supporting Nasser's demand that King Faisal of oil-rich Saudi Arabia spend more of his country's enormous oil wealth on seeking the annihilation of Israel. Qaddafi charged that Faisal's extensive dealings with the American companies extracting oil from his nation had in fact led him to favor Israel in the Middle Eastern conflict. He repeated this accusation to reporters gathered outside the conference. The other rulers were offended not only by the content of his statements but even more by his rough and arrogant manner. President Houari Boumédienne of Algeria had the tacit support of every Arab leader when he told Qaddafi that

Qaddafi became the Libyan prime minister in January 1970. His true power, however, derived from his position as the chairman of the Revolutionary Command Council, which could dismiss the prime minister and all other members of the cabinet, or Council of Ministers.

AP/WIDE WORLD PHOTOS

AP/WIDE WORLD PHOTOS

Faisal ibn Saud reigned as king of Saudi Arabia from 1964 to 1975 and succeeded in translating his nation's ownership of the world's largest oil reserves into tremendous wealth and power. His moderate regime incurred Qaddafi's wrath by not contributing more to the struggle against Israel.

he was "a child who does not know what he is talking about." When Qaddafi reported on the conference to the RCC he was literally in tears over his failure to endear himself to other Muslim leaders.

Shortly after his return to Libya, Qaddafi was struck by an attack of appendicitis. He was rushed to the hospital and operated on immediately. While in the hospital recovering from the surgery, he was attended by a beautiful young nurse named Safia. Though he had only recently been married, Qaddafi quickly fell in love with Safia. In keeping with the rules of his Muslim religion, he divorced his first wife, Fathia. He then married Safia, who has since borne him six children. Only six months had elapsed between his two weddings.

During his first year in power, Qaddafi moved quickly not only in marital affairs but in foreign affairs as well. His foreign policy seemed to mirror that of Nasser. Its primary goals were to foster Arab unity by extending political cooperation with other Arab states, to restore an Arab state in Palestine by providing logistical and financial support for Arab wars against Israel, and to reject all attempts by the superpowers to make Libya their satellite. But Qaddafi added a new wrinkle. In 1970 he launched a campaign to finance what he called "independence movements" throughout the world. "One should not consider the traditional outdated excuse about interference in the internal affairs of others," he announced in mid-1970. It was a warning. The steps the new Libyan ruler took following the announcement shocked many Western governments.

Qaddafi shipped arms to the Irish Republican Army for use against the British in Northern Ireland and equipped Muslim rebels against the Philippine government. He financed various revolutionary groups in Central and South America, and he even sent $300,000 to the Black Panthers, a group of American blacks that was attempting through violent means to disrupt the United States government and to establish a separate black nation. There seemed to be no logic or pattern to the campaign except that it provided funds to violent, radical groups. In fact, many of the recipients had conflicting ideologies.

Another of Qaddafi's early goals as leader was to reduce foreign economic and political influence over Libya. In October 1969 he began pressuring for the removal of the American and British military installations. On October 28 the RCC decreed that the United States had to evacuate Wheelus Air Force Base by December 24, 1970. The base was formally turned over to Libya on June 11, 1970. The British withdrew the last of their troops on March 31, 1970, amid nationwide nationalist rallies. Qaddafi used the vacated American base to strengthen military ties with Egypt. Nasser had previously agreed to provide military officers to run Qaddafi's program to retrain the Libyan army. In exchange for this favor, Qaddafi gave Egypt the American base — replete with a squadron of Mirage fighter-bombers purchased from France. Qaddafi's ultimate intent in making this deal was to augment Egypt's military strength for the ongoing struggle against Israel. Qaddafi also took steps to gain more control over the Libyan oil industry. Seeking to increase Libya's oil wealth, Qaddafi on two occasions imposed large increases in the prices that U.S. and European companies paid for Libyan oil.

Meanwhile, the RCC was beginning to improve the general quality of life in the country, though economic planning continued to be disorganized. It built roads, hospitals, and schools and started programs to irrigate the desert and increase the amount of arable land. Power lines were strung

A solitary oil rig is dwarfed by the gentle curves of the vast Libyan desert. By the time Qaddafi took power in September 1969, Libya had become the world's fourth largest oil exporter — in part because of its proximity to Europe. Over the course of his first three years in power, Qaddafi would nationalize 51 percent of the assets of all foreign oil companies operating in Libya.

UPI/BETTMANN NEWSPHOTOS

Some members of the Black Panther party demonstrate outside an Oakland, California courthouse, during the 1968 trial of their leader, Huey Newton. This black nationalist organization was one of the many radical groups that Qaddafi funded in his extensive — seemingly indiscriminate — campaign for "national liberation."

UPI/RETTMANN NEWSPHOTOS

through the desert to bring electricity to remote areas. Until Qaddafi took power, most Bedouins did not have access to electricity. Not having sufficient power to drive pumping machines, they were forced, among other hardships, to carry water in buckets over great distances. Qaddafi hoped that one day the Bedouins might even be able to watch their leader speak on television.

In one of his regular bouts of insecurity, Qaddafi wondered if the people approved of his programs. In order to find out, he disguised himself in the robes of a Bedouin sheepherder and traveled to some of the remote desert villages, where people were unlikely to recognize him. He sat around campfires with camel drivers and goat breeders and struggling farmers and asked casual questions to find out how they felt about things. The young Qaddafa Berber tribesman was pleased to learn that they approved of their new leader.

In the cities Qaddafi did not enjoy the same unqualified support. Wandering the streets of Tripoli after dark in a poor man's caftan with a hood that hid his face, he heard grumblings about the way things had been going since he came to power. He heard complaints about the loss of revenue that resulted when the foreign military bases were closed and the free-spending British and American personnel departed. In addition, urban unemployment was on the rise. There was anger at the closure of taverns and at new legislation against jeans and long hair. Women resented the new government's laws concerning skirt lengths, laws which policemen enforced by marking with indelible ink the legs of women whose hemlines fell too high.

Like many leaders firmly entrenched in power, Qaddafi quickly developed a thick skin against criticism. He had the faith of a religious zealot, convinced that his leadership of Libya had divine sanction. He never doubted his own greatness. And so it was that late one night he sent a messenger to ask the French ambassador to come to the military compound in which the Qaddafi family lived.

Qaddafi had decided that he was the modern Arab equivalent of the 19th-century French leader Napoleon Bonaparte, who had become legendary through a series of spectacular military victories but who ultimately had squandered France's material and human resources under the arrogant delusion that he could rule all of Europe. Qaddafi hoped that eventually his own name would become synonymous with the state of Libya — in the same way

American jets being refueled at Wheelus Air Force Base near Tripoli. Qaddafi forced the U.S. to give up this important military base in 1970. Nevertheless, because of Qaddafi's virulent anticommunism, the U.S. continued to support him in the early 1970s—even providing CIA protection.

AP/WIDE WORLD PHOTOS

French citizens had seen Napoleon as the embodiment of French glory. He hoped that when he spoke, it would be as the voice of all Libyans. He asked the French ambassador to confirm this fantasy. "Napoleon," Qaddafi said when the ambassador stood before him. "Tell me what you know of him. I want to understand Napoleon."

In his arrogance, Qaddafi imagined a parallel between Napoleon's role in 19th-century Europe and his own in the modern Middle East. Just as Napoleon had once tried to harness the zeal of opposition groups in neighboring countries to form a European union dominated by France, Qaddafi hoped eventually to form a confederation of Arab states led by Libya. It was a long-range goal, but one that Qaddafi would periodically make efforts to achieve.

But in 1970, as Qaddafi continued to have difficulty establishing friendly relationships with other

Shoppers in a crowded market in Tripoli haggle over the price of imported shoes. Qaddafi significantly improved the standard of living in Libya by imposing several price hikes on foreign oil companies and nationalizing the majority of their assets. The resultant wealth was spread among the entire population. By 1977 the per capita income would be $6,451, the highest on the African continent.

AP/WIDE WORLD PHOTOS

AP/WIDE WORLD PHOTOS

Arab leaders, Arab unity remained an idle dream. His second visit to an Arab summit proved as disastrous as his first. It was made one full year after he had come to power, at a September 1970 summit conference in Cairo. His behavior turned out to be not only undiplomatic but actually insulting to the other Middle Eastern heads of state.

The summit had been called in an attempt to defuse the burgeoning conflict in Jordan between the Palestine Liberation Organization (PLO) and Jordanian government troops. For many years, Jordan had provided a haven for Arab refugees from the territory controlled by Israel. The Palestinians had been first uprooted during the 1948–49 Arab-Israeli war, during which Israel had expanded its territory to include most of what the UN had designated as the Arab portion of Palestine. Some refugees had fled following the 1967 Arab-Israeli War (the Six-Day War) during which the Jordanian territory known as the West Bank was lost to Israel. By 1970, refugee

Colonel Qaddafi cultivated the image not only of a desert nomad but also of a military hero — fashioning himself as a modern-day Napoleon. Here, resplendent in his dress uniform, he announces that he will send aid to the Irish Republican Army (IRA), the Catholic terrorist group fighting for British withdrawal from Northern Ireland.

Gamal Abdel Nasser (right) with Yasir Arafat, the chairman of the Palestine Liberation Organization (PLO). Arafat helped to organize Arab refugees, stranded by the formation of a Jewish state in Palestine, into a guerrilla army and a potent political force. Qaddafi has been a diehard supporter of the Palestinian cause, establishing a "holy war" fund in early 1970.

camps stretched along the entire western frontier of Jordan, and Palestinian poverty had become a growing drag on the Jordanian economy. In addition, the area had become a base for military forays into Israel by the Palestinians' guerrilla army, the PLO, which under the leadership of its chairman, Yasir Arafat, sought to recapture Palestine. After Jordan had suffered several retaliatory attacks by Israel for PLO raids, Jordan's leader, King Hussein, decided to drive the PLO from his country.

To Qaddafi, Hussein's action constituted treason. Qaddafi not only criticized Hussein's expulsion of the Palestinians but also suggested to the Arab leaders gathered at Cairo's Nile Hotel that they commit forces to the PLO's fight against the Jordanians.

Standing up at the meeting, waving a revolver about wildly, he suggested that he himself march at the front of the proposed Arab force.

Clearly, Qaddafi lacked Nasser's diplomatic skills. Moderate states, such as Saudi Arabia, rejected the proposal. Even several Arab leaders who had been deeply offended by Hussein's action had no interest in waging war against a fellow Arab ruler. Hussein was the legitimate leader of an autonomous nation. No matter how sympathetic they might feel toward the Palestinian refugees, the PLO was still a band of irregulars whose confused lines of authority sometimes made them behave like outlaws.

Qaddafi was infuriated by the other leaders' condescending attitude in rejecting his proposal. Only Nasser was able to calm him down. Everybody could see that holding back his fiery young Libyan protégé

Colonel Muammar el-Qaddafi has pursued Arab unity with singular fervor, turning Libya into a suitor whose persistence only repels less ardent Arab states.

—from a report published by the Congressional Quarterly Inc.

AP/WIDE WORLD PHOTOS

King Hussein of Jordan. In September 1970 Hussein took military action to rid his country of Palestinian guerrilla bases in an attempt to forestall Israeli retaliatory attacks on his country. At the Arab peace meeting in Cairo that same month, a revolver-toting Qaddafi raged against Hussein's "treachery."

Mourners struggle to touch Nasser's flag-draped coffin as his funeral cortege passes through Cairo. Nasser's death on September 28, 1970, came as a heavy blow to Qaddafi, whose political viewpoints and programs were largely adapted from the Egyptian president's Islamic socialism.

UPI/BETTMANN NEWSPHOTOS

> ***What Qaddafi serves up is a mishmash of half-baked ideology and romantic idealism. Surely he himself must be too shrewd to take it seriously.***
>
> —EDOUARD SAAB
> Lebanese editor and journalist

was a great strain on the Egyptian president.

During the conference, rumors circulated that Nasser was ill. Less than a week later, on September 28, 1970, Gamal Abdel Nasser, the statesman Qaddafi so idolized, the revolutionary leader he patterned himself after, died.

Nasser was succeeded as president of Egypt by Anwar Sadat, a 52-year-old military officer who had been his vice-president. Under Sadat, domestic conditions in Egypt would change, as would the balance of power in the Middle East and the state of Libyan-Egyptian relations. There would be many twists and turns in Sadat's relations with other countries (particularly with Israel) over the years that followed, but from the start his actions were guided by a single underlying precept.

The precept was that Egypt had been damaged by its antipathy toward Israel, that it had become a prisoner to a policy that chained it to the Soviets, alienated it from the Americans, and depressed its economy. Sadat decided to try to change that situation. He knew that in order to do so, Egypt would ultimately have to compromise with Israel in ways that all Arab states had vowed never to do.

Sadat's revolutionary change in position would soon lead Qaddafi to determine that Egypt was Libya's worst enemy, and that its president, Anwar Sadat, was the devil that he must destroy.

Though Qaddafi (left) was grief-stricken by Nasser's death, he persisted in his obsessive quest for Arab unity. On November 6, 1970, he met with Egypt's new president, Anwar Sadat (center), and the Sudan's Gaafer al-Nimeiry to mark the official end of mourning for Nasser. Two days later, the three leaders met again to "coordinate the policies of the three countries."

UPI/BETTMANN NEWSPHOTOS

4

The Quest for Arab Unity

> ***In the medium and short runs . . . you might even say that for Israel, Qaddafi can be a kind of asset. Who else, in all his frantic attempts to unite the Arabs, is keeping them divided to the extent Qaddafi is? He is a strategic threat but perhaps a tactical asset; an agent of division in the Arab world.***
>
> —Israeli intelligence chief

Like his role model, Napoleon, Qaddafi became increasingly tyrannical during the course of his rule. His first taste of power only whetted his appetite for more. It inspired him to make his power absolute. It insured his corruption.

There is no room for opposition to such leadership, and so, on June 11, 1971, Qaddafi took steps to silence all who disagreed with his policies. He instituted the death penalty for those who engaged in political activity against him. Editors and reporters who worked for newspapers that opposed him were arrested and jailed. Strikes were forbidden, and workers who stayed away from their jobs faced prison terms for "absenteeism." Qaddafi established the Arab Socialist Union (ASU) in 1972 as Libya's only political party.

To secure the allegiance of the people, Qaddafi skillfully created a public image of himself as a devout and simple man. He conducted state business in a tent behind Tripoli's Bab al-Azzizia barracks, where his wife and children lived. He drank camel's milk and lunched on coarse Berber bread. He went

After Nasser's death, Qaddafi strove to replace the Egyptian president as the undisputed leader of the Arab world. He paid homage to Nasser by founding a mass political organization modeled after Egypt's Arab Socialist Union (ASU). Under Qaddafi, the ASU was established as Libya's sole political party.

AP/WIDE WORLD PHOTOS

AP/WIDE WORLD PHOTOS

This juxtaposition of a gleaming new mosque (an Islamic place of worship) with a Tripoli oil company office (left) suggests the divergent forces of economic modernization and cultural conservatism at work in Qaddafi's Libya. Hundreds of public structures — including hospitals, mosques, schools, and public housing — have been built by the Qaddafi regime.

to the desert and slept under the stars. He prayed with the Bedouins five times a day. Only in the desert, he said, could he truly find food for his spirit. His roots were in the Libyan soil. Age-old family and tribal values had shaped his character. He believed that he patterned himself after the man he most admired in history — "Ibrahim" Lincoln. Like Lincoln, he said, he would always be a simple man of the people. To demonstrate his humility, Qaddafi announced that henceforth he was to be called simply "Brother Colonel."

But for those who knew him in private, he was anything but simple. Beneath his haughty manner, he was plagued by confusion and self-doubt and given to dark moods and periods of brooding. He suffered from chronic insomnia, which he often attempted to relieve by driving his car late at night at top speeds over the winding desert roads just outside Tripoli. Dawn would find him haggard and windblown, the engine of his vehicle fiery from its ordeal.

His depressions became so intense that, on several occasions, he admitted himself for treatment at

There is absolutely no question of whether Qaddafi really believes his own rhetoric; he does.

—JOHN K. COOLEY
American journalist

Egyptian sanatoriums. There were rumors that he had received drug treatments to ease his tensions at an institution in northern Italy. Once, two British specialists were flown into Tripoli to consult with Libyan physicians on how best to stabilize Brother Colonel's mood swings.

These problems were, of course, kept secret. In public Qaddafi appeared strong, sure of himself, always in control. This was particularly true in his dealings with the foreign oil companies.

By threatening to nationalize Libya's oil fields, refineries, and shipping facilities, Qaddafi forced the foreign petroleum companies to agree to pay 35 percent more for his country's oil. This, on top of the previous increases he had forced on them and changes in the world oil market resulting from the 1973 Arab-Israeli war and the increased marketing aggressiveness of the OPEC (Organization of Petroleum Exporting Countries) nations, pushed up the price of oil all over the world. The increase was felt particularly in the United States, where petroleum importers balked at paying the high prices. The re-

AP/WIDE WORLD PHOTOS

Libyan children wear guerrilla uniforms and wield toy weapons at an anti-American rally. Though under Qaddafi such outbursts of nationalistic fervor were common, particularly among desert dwellers and the urban poor, more cosmopolitan elements of society resented his strict regulation of morality.

sulting shortage of gasoline caused long lines at fuel pumps from Maine to California. Soon car drivers were paying four and five times the former price per gallon of gas—when they could get it.

A short time after the 35 percent increase was agreed to, Qaddafi demanded a "surtax" on top of it. The foreign companies were outraged. They refused at first to give in to the additional demand. But when Qaddafi shut down the Shell Oil terminals, they once again gave him what he wanted.

AP/WIDE WORLD PHOTOS

Yasir Arafat shows his approval of young guerrilla troops who have graduated from a Palestinian training camp in Syria. Convinced that Arafat would betray the Palestinians by negotiating with Israel, Qaddafi set up his own camps in the Libyan desert in 1972 and staffed them with dissident members of the PLO.

Nor was that the only instance of Qaddafi using Libya's oil to exert pressure on Western nations. In December 1971 Qaddafi had asked for yet another price increase. Again the companies refused. In the name of the Libyan government, Qaddafi seized the oil fields and processing plants owned by British Petroleum. The other companies, the majority of them American, once again granted an increase.

Then Qaddafi shocked the West even further by negotiating a deal that seemed to contradict his professed anticommunism. He made an arrangement allowing the Soviet Union to extract oil from the nationalized British Petroleum fields in exchange for weapons and planes. Libyan oil had always been available to the Western democracies. Now, for the first time, it was available to communist nations as well. Qaddafi had thumbed his nose at the west — particularly at the United States. Indeed, by September 1973, Qaddafi had nationalized 51 percent of the assets of all foreign oil companies operating in Libya.

Qaddafi was especially eager to obtain sophisticated Soviet weaponry and aircraft in order to strengthen his forces for an increasingly interventionist foreign policy. He had decided that if the other Arab leaders would not act to protect the Palestinians from King Hussein's Jordanian army, he would do so alone. He sent 300 Libyan "volunteers" to aid the PLO guerrillas. (He also offered to send Libyan troops to help the Jordanian army depose King Hussein and aided an assassination plot against the king to prove he was serious. The plot failed.)

At the same time, Qaddafi was trying to overthrow

the government of Morocco. He helped finance a coup against Morocco's leader, King Hassan II, and when it did not succeed, he openly financed a rebel group called the Polisarios in their Soviet-supported war against the Moroccan government. "The best thing that could happen in Morocco would be the death of the king," he announced to the world.

In similar fashion, Qaddafi meddled in the internal affairs of two of his North African neighbors, Chad and the Sudan. Farther from home, he continued to supply Muslim rebels in the Philippines, agitated for a holy war by Pakistani Muslims against India, and contributed money to a variety of radical groups in the United States. Among these was the Symbionese Liberation Army, an obscure extremist group with a nebulous plan for revolution that became known to the world when it kidnapped heiress Patricia Hearst and forced her to join in a series of random acts of violence that culminated in a bank holdup and murder.

In early 1972, sure that he could continue to trade Libyan oil for the Soviet armaments that would be needed, Qaddafi started a program for training Arab revolutionaries for action throughout the Middle East. He said he would turn Libya into "a school where we will teach how a people can take up arms to stage a revolution." He recruited Arab militants, many of them still in their teens, from all over the Middle East. Trainees included members of the Black September group (a dissident PLO faction that took its name from the September 1970 attacks by Jordanian troops on the Palestinian refugee camps).

Qaddafi set up training camps deep in the Libyan Desert with the aim of turning these raw recruits into a disciplined team of commando-style terrorists. He hired former officers from the East German, Polish, and Egyptian militaries to run the camps. Qaddafi called his new paramilitary force "National Arab Youth for the Liberation of Palestine" (NAYLP). He put the staunch Black Septembrist Ahmed al-Ghaffour, a former aide of PLO leader Yasir Arafat, in charge of the NAYLP. For the first time, a terrorist group had the formal and substantial backing of a

AP/WIDE WORLD PHOTOS

King Hassan II of Morocco reassures the world that he is safe, following a thwarted coup attempt financed by Qaddafi. Ninety-two people were killed as military cadets raided Hassan's summer palace at the beach resort of Skhirat on July 11, 1971. Hassan escaped harm by locking himself in a toilet.

AP/WIDE WORLD PHOTOS

When Anwar Sadat (right) first met Qaddafi in 1970, he found him "an eye-catching character with a revolver that never left his belt." Here, in April 1971, the two leaders are all smiles as they negotiate political union between their nations. Relations between Libya and Egypt would later sour.

country's government and its leader.

European countries had learned their first lesson about Qaddafi's willingness to use force and intimidation from an incident in the summer of 1971 involving a British passenger plane. Among its passengers, the plane carried two leaders of an unsuccessful coup attempt against President Gaafer al-Nimeiry of Sudan, at that time a Qaddafi ally. At Qaddafi's order, Libyan fighter planes forced the craft to the ground. The two Sudanese plotters were arrested and returned to their country. Qaddafi detained the plane's crew and passengers for hours, long enough to inspire a flood of international protests and to show the world that he was a force to be reckoned with. He was satisfied that he had made his point.

Qaddafi's obsessive quest for Arab unity finally produced tangible results on April 17, 1971, when Egypt, Libya, and Syria agreed to form a political union called the Federation of Arab Republics. On September 1, referenda were held in the three countries, and citizens voted almost unanimously to approve a constitution drawn up by the three heads of state: Qaddafi, Egyptian President Anwar Sadat, and Syrian President Hafez al-Assad. The leaders met again in Cairo on October 4 to finalize the pact, naming Sadat as the federation's first president and choosing Cairo as its capital. While on paper the federation appeared to conjoin the three states — setting up a presidential council, a joint court system, and an assembly — in actuality it only implied a loose political cooperation. The new state was to come into being on January 1, 1972.

The next year Egypt and Libya decided to go beyond the federation and actually merge their states. Qaddafi proposed "total union" on July 27, 1972,

> ***The key factor, of course, is oil. It supplies the wealth that Qaddafi redistributes.***
> —DOYLE MCMANUS
> American journalist

AP/WIDE WORLD PHOTOS

Hafez al-Assad, president of Syria. Assad, Sadat, and Qaddafi agreed on April 17, 1971, to form the Federation of Arab Republics. The federation among Syria, Libya, and Egypt was officially to come into being on January 1, 1972, and was to be a loose political confederation.

UPI/BETTMANN NEWSPHOTOS

Sadat (far left, seated), Qaddafi (with hat, seated), and Assad (far right, seated) sign the papers establishing the Federation of Arab Republics. Five months after this meeting, Sadat and Qaddafi agreed to go beyond the cooperation implied by the federation and fully merge their nations by September 1973.

soon after Sadat had expelled Soviet military advisers from Egypt, a move that appealed to the Libyan leader's anticommunism. On August 2, 1972, the two leaders signed an agreement vowing to "create a unified state and to establish a unified political command to bring about in stages the merger of the two countries by September 1, 1973." In the new state, Sadat was to become president and Qaddafi was to be vice-president and head of the armed forces. But when the two met on September 18 to discuss the first steps toward unification, Sadat told Qaddafi he opposed the Libyan's appointment as commander in chief because Egypt had historically had problems when politicians became involved in the military. Qaddafi assented. The pace of the merger was to be gradual so as not to be unfair to oil-rich Libya, which would contribute far more money than Egypt to the scheme. It was agreed that joint committees would be formed to draw up a new constitution, to coordinate economic policies, and to create an assembly.

Of course, Libya is a base for us, and a very important one to the Palestinian cause.
—BILAL ABU JIHAD
leader of the Palestine Popular Struggle Front

Over the course of the ensuing year, however, Egyptian-Libyan relations would sour, and in an August 1973 meeting, held right before the scheduled deadline for the union's completion, a new agreement was signed, calling for a much slower process of integration. Ultimately, the Federation of Arab Republics and the Egyptian-Libyan collaboration were abandoned, for a number of reasons. Throughout 1973 the question of Israel severely strained relations between Libya and Egypt. First Sadat refused to participate in Qaddafi's aggressive schemes against the Jewish state, then Sadat attacked Israel without involving Qaddafi in the decision. Eventually, Sadat committed what was to Qaddafi the ultimate sin — negotiating peace. In addition, the personalities of the two leaders did not mesh well. As the two countries later approached a state of war, the Libyan press would describe Sadat and his wife as a "20th-century Antony and Cleopatra," and Sadat would reply that Qaddafi was "100 percent sick and possessed of the devil." Further reasons for the dissolution of the merger are suggested by the American journalist John K. Cooley: "The [joint] committees were bureaucratic by nature . . . the abilities of many of the committee members were limited . . . the two countries were fundamentally different, and xenophobia was rife."

In the summer of 1972 an unrelated event captured the attention of all Muslim leaders, and of the leaders of the rest of the world as well. On September 5, Arab terrorists breached the security of the Olympic Games being held in Munich, West Germany, and seized as hostages several members of the Israeli team, killing two of them. After a long process of negotiations, the terrorists killed the remaining nine Israeli hostages. Libya was implicated in the action. Weapons used by the terrorists had been smuggled into Germany via Libyan embassy diplo-

UPI/BETTMANN NEWSPHOTOS

Libyan students hail the Federation of Arab Republics with a banner that reads "Arab unity is our road to victory." Their enthusiasm quickly dissipated as the federation was undermined by cultural differences between member nations and the incompatible temperaments of Sadat and Qaddafi.

matic pouches. Moreover, while the terrorists were holed up in the rooms of their hostages at the Olympic Village in Munich, they had placed two phone calls to a high-ranking Tunisian government official later revealed to be on Qaddafi's payroll. When five of the terrorists were killed by West German police, Qaddafi eulogized the Arabs as "martyr heroes" and had their bodies flown to Tripoli for burial with full military honors. Later, when three of the captured terrorists escaped to Libya, Qaddafi granted them sanctuary and refused to return them to Germany to stand trial. For the first time, Qaddafi had stepped into the full spotlight of world attention. Most of those watching were appalled.

UPI/BETTMANN NEWSPHOTOS

The spirit of friendly competition at the 1972 Summer Olympic Games in Munich, West Germany, was shattered when Palestinian commandos took over an Israeli dormitory. These weightlifters and eight other Israeli athletes were killed by the terrorists. For the first time, Qaddafi was linked to a major terrorist action.

5

The People's Revolution

> ***Those who direct the course of life for themselves do not need to watch it working through actors on the stage or in the cinemas.***
>
> —MUAMMAR EL-QADDAFI

Qaddafi's role in the Olympic massacre labeled him an enemy in the eyes of Israel. On February 21, 1973, Israel exacted its revenge when a Libyan passenger plane bound for Cairo, Egypt, drifted off course and crossed the Israeli border. Israeli pursuit planes attacked the jetliner. The Libyan pilot radioed the Egyptians for help. Although the Egyptians had a nearby air base with jet fighters on constant alert, they took no action. The Libyan craft was destroyed and all 108 people aboard died.

Enraged, Qaddafi demanded an explanation from Sadat for the Egyptian failure to support an Arab ally against an Israeli attack. Sadat told him that the Egyptian fighter planes had been grounded because of "bad weather." Qaddafi responded angrily that the weather had not been bad enough to keep the Israelis on the ground.

Qaddafi asked Sadat to cooperate with Libya in a retaliatory bombing strike against Israel. Sadat refused. Disgusted, the Libyan leader told his people that their neighbors were nothing but "cowardly Egyptians."

In 1973 Qaddafi became increasingly isolated in the Arab world as a result of his association with Palestinian terrorists and his involvement in plots to assassinate Sadat. On the domestic front, he launched a cultural revolution that called for an overhaul of the legal system and an ideological campaign to eliminate "intellectual perverts" from Libya.

AP/WIDE WORLD PHOTOS

UPI/BETTMANN NEWSPHOTOS

An Israeli soldier stands guard over the charred wreckage of a Libyan commercial airliner that was shot down by Israel on February 21, 1973, killing all 108 passengers. The Libyan Airlines jet had reportedly failed to heed Israeli instructions to land after straying over the Israeli-occupied Sinai. Sadat's refusal to send Egyptian jet fighters to the aid of the Libyan airliner incensed Qaddafi.

Nevertheless, Qaddafi was determined to strike back. He saw his opportunity when he learned that, for the occasion of Israel's 25th anniversary as a nation, a group of wealthy American and European Jews had arranged to sail to the Holy Land on the world's most renowned and luxurious ocean liner, the *Queen Elizabeth II*. The *QE II* was to leave Southampton, England, on April 15 and dock in Israel on May 15.

At this time, under the federation's joint defense agreement, Egyptian submarines used Libyan ports to refuel and while docked there were technically under Libyan command. Qaddafi summoned the captain of one of these vessels to his headquarters. He ordered him to intercept and sink the *Queen Elizabeth II* as it sailed across the Mediterranean to Israel. The captain, aware of the gravity of the order, asked his Libyan superior to put it in writing. Qaddafi did so.

Still, the Egyptian naval officer had grave doubts. As soon as his ship was out of Libyan waters, he radioed Cairo and asked that his Egyptian superiors confirm Qaddafi's order. Sadat spoke personally to the submarine commander and told him that under no circumstances was he to sink the *Queen Elizabeth II*. Instead, the sub commander was to inform Qaddafi that he had lost the *Queen Elizabeth II* in heavy fog. Weather reports revealed no such fog, but Qaddafi did not make an issue of it.

The Libyan leader did not, however, give up on the idea of revenge. Convinced that Israel's existence depended on continued support from its Western allies, especially the United States, he decided to wage war on Zionism by attempting to undermine Israel's relationships with those allies. This would be done by targeting for terrorist attacks citizens of governments with policies Qaddafi determined to be pro-Israel.

He is moody. If you do not satisfy him, you get a kick.
—ABU AYAD
Palestine Liberation Organization leader, on Qaddafi

The first action reflecting this new strategy took place on August 5, 1973, at the Athens airport, when passengers checking in at a flight desk were strafed by machine-gun fire. Three were killed and fifty-five were wounded. The attack had been carried out by members of the National Arab Youth for the Liberation of Palestine — the NAYLP — graduates of the Libyan commando training camps.

Four months later, on December 17, the NAYLP hit the Rome airport in an incident that the world labeled a "massacre." Thirty-two people were killed, eighteen were wounded, and a plane was hijacked. When the hijackers were apprehended, one of them told the authorities that Qaddafi had personally ordered the slaughter, and that it had been carried

Wealthy American and European Jews, bound from Southampton, England, to the Holy Land to celebrate Israel's 25th anniversary, board the ocean liner *Queen Elizabeth II* on April 15, 1973. Sadat thwarted Qaddafi's plan to have a Tripoli-based Egyptian submarine attack the British ship.

AP/WIDE WORLD PHOTOS

He is a man with a single purpose: the destruction of Israel.

—Israeli intelligence chief, on Qaddafi

out after Qaddafi's original plan, the assassination of U.S. Secretary of State Henry Kissinger, had been foiled by U.S. intelligence agents.

Meanwhile, on the domestic front, Qaddafi noticed what he thought was a lack of popular enthusiasm for his regime's programs. Few Libyans had chosen to enlist in the all-volunteer Libyan army; participation in new agricultural and industrial projects was disappointingly low; and universities were, in Qaddafi's view, swarming with "perverts" who opposed his rule. To treat this apparent malaise, Qaddafi instituted a "people's revolution." This revolution would ultimately result in sweeping changes to the Libyan economic and political structures. On April 15, 1973, which was the Muslim holy day commemorating the birthday of the Prophet Muhammad, the Libyan leader announced a five-point reform program:

1. The existing legal system was to be abolished and replaced with Muslim law.
2. The "political illnesses" of the country were to be cured by banishing communists, atheists, and "deviationists."

UPI/BETTMANN NEWSPHOTOS

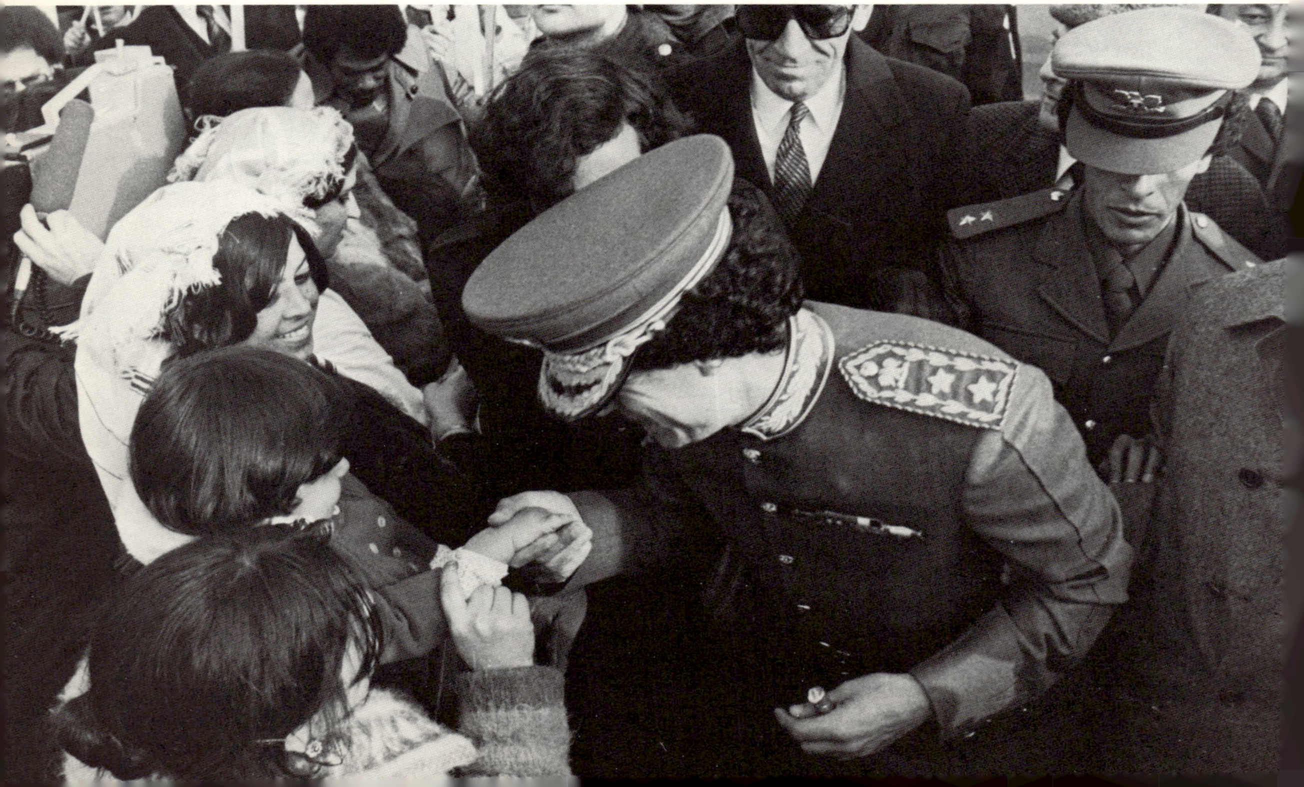

Qaddafi mingles with young admirers. In what he claimed was an attempt to give power to the Libyan people, Qaddafi in April 1973 instituted his "people's revolution." According to a five-point program, all laws in force were to be replaced by Muslim religious law; dangerous ideologies, including communism, were to be purged; all citizens were to be armed; bureaucracy was to be trimmed; and universities were to be reorganized.

3. All loyal citizens were to be armed.
4. The bureaucracy of the government was to be "revolutionized" and "procrastinators" were to be fired.
5. A cultural revolution was to be launched on college campuses to eliminate dissident forces and to purge the curriculum of unacceptable ideologies.

Throughout 1973 and 1974, steps were taken to transform the political system into what Qaddafi called a "direct democracy." All Libyans became members of the government as participants in local popular congresses, political bodies organized for each neighborhood, village, workplace, and university. The primary function of these congresses was to appoint and oversee "people's committees" that assumed the responsibilities of preexisting local governments, providing basic services like education, housing, water, and electricity. People's committees passed on information about the needs of villages and families to regional committees and to the national leadership and also started "executive action" on programs conceived at higher levels. Plans were also made for a new national legislature to be called the General People's Congress (GPC) and to be made up of representatives of the congresses and committees. The GPC, which would hold the first of its annual sessions in November 1976, was ostensibly to make final decisions on major policy subjects. In reality this meant determining such things as new directions in agricultural and energy policy. More important decisions continued to be made by the Revolutionary Command Council (RCC), which in 1977 would be renamed the General Secretariat of the GPC.

The new political arrangement reflected general precepts for running government that Qaddafi would outline in *The Green Book, Vol. 1: the Solution of the Problem of Democracy*, published in 1975. This tract, which purported to present "the final solution to the problem of the instrument of governing," was the first of three volumes in which Qaddafi set forth his plan for the ideal society; the volumes together were intended to serve as "the new

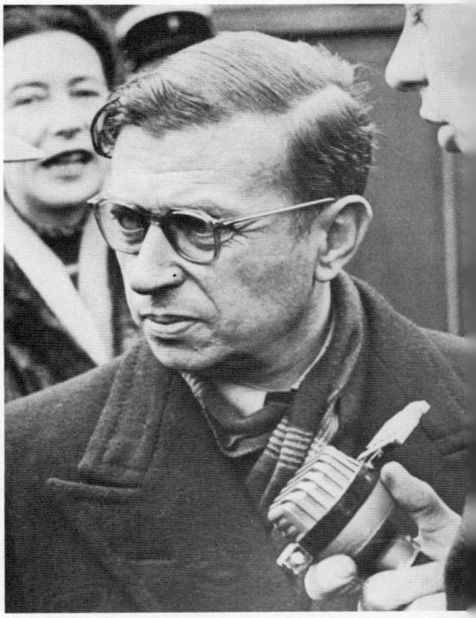

UPI/BETTMANN NEWSPHOTOS

Jean-Paul Sartre — philosopher, novelist, dramatist, and critic — was a leading figure in French existentialism, a postwar philosophical movement that emphasized personal freedom in an uncertain and purposeless world. Sartre's works, including *Nausea* and *Being and Nothingness*, were considered dangerously atheistic in Libya and were publicly burned.

On April 6, 1974, the Libyan Foreign Ministry announced that Qaddafi would be relieved of his ceremonial, political, and administrative functions and that Major Abdel Salem Jalloud (right) would assume them. Though the move was thought at first to signal a major shift in the Libyan balance of power, it in fact represented a mere transfer of titles.

AP/WIDE WORLD PHOTOS

Nobody is poor. Everyone has a house or an apartment. I've got a car, because I've got a job and a salary. Ten or even five years ago, no one could have guaranteed me any of these things. Now they're guaranteed to everyone.

—official Libyan guide, in 1974

gospel, the gospel of the new era, the era of the masses." In the first volume, Qaddafi describes how, in his view, all previous attempts at democracy have failed. To Qaddafi, all governments that involve parliaments, electoral systems, votes, and referenda are actually dictatorships by the majority. If in one of these "false democracies" a candidate wins 51 percent of the vote, Qaddafi explains, "49 percent of the electorate is ruled by an instrument of governing they did not vote for." Qaddafi also faults typical democracies for forcing their citizens to forfeit power to representatives. According to a slogan printed in green in the margin of the book and seen on posters throughout Libya, "representation is a denial of participation." To Qaddafi, the most desirable form of government involves all citizens. Such a system prevents any one faction — group, party, tribe, or class — from taking complete control, which, says Qaddafi, is the natural result in most democracies. Only at the end of the book does Qaddafi attempt to explain the apparent contradiction of, on the one hand, instituting "direct democracy," and on the other hand, continuing to exercise dictatorial control over most key decisions. While theoretically "direct democracy" is ideal, he writes, in reality the strong always rule — "the stronger part in the society is the one that rules."

Even as *The Green Book* was being written, Qaddafi's rule was becoming increasingly repressive and his people's committees were becoming more and more powerful. Under his prodding they engaged in a round of public book-burnings that saw works by such authors as Henry James, Graham Greene, and Jean-Paul Sartre go up in flames. Qaddafi's secret police continued to arrest those who opposed his policies. The people's committees began to persecute those whom Qaddafi labeled as "intellectuals."

But there was no public outcry. The average Libyan citizen, preoccupied with the daily struggle to survive, was not displeased with Qaddafi's rule. The quality of life and the standard of living had definitely improved under him. The irrigation projects were beginning to have an effect and crops thrived in several parts of the desert. Electricity was available to five times as many Libyans as under King Idris I. More and more people had television sets and even cars.

It was not only an increase in the availability of consumer goods, but also Qaddafi's style that made

All important matters are supposed to be discussed until a consensus is reached. Anyone still opposing that consensus once it is reached ultimately becomes a dissident, an outcast, and an enemy of the state.

—JOHN K. COOLEY
American journalist, on the Revolutionary Command Council

An Israeli column moving toward the Sinai front passes a truckload of captured Egyptian soldiers during the 1967 Six-Day War. Since the United Nations partitioned Palestine into separate Jewish and Arab states in 1947, there have been five Arab-Israeli wars.

UPI/BETTMANN NEWSPHOTOS

During the 1973 Arab-Israeli War, an Israeli soldier cautiously patrols the tense Gaza Strip — a 35-mile sliver of Mediterranean coastline captured by Israel from Egypt in 1967. Hostilities broke out on October 6, 1973, the Jewish holy day of Yom Kippur. Qaddafi contributed a squadron of Mirage fighter planes, 100 armored personnel carriers, and approximately $500 million to the Arab cause.

AP/WIDE WORLD PHOTOS

him popular. An expert at manipulating public opinion, Qaddafi continually staged events designed to prove to his people that he was just a simple Arab like them. In the summer of 1973, for instance, he resigned from his post as leader of the Revolutionary Command Council. He personally handed out copies of his resignation on the streets of Tripoli. "I continue to work . . . to lead the masses to assume their right in power," he assured his fellow Libyans. By this shrewd move, Qaddafi managed to endear himself to the antiestablishment young people whose numbers were increasing rapidly throughout the country.

To the young, Qaddafi played the role of the tender romantic. "I am a poet," he told reporters. Sometimes, he added, "I weep, but only when I am alone." Brother Colonel soon had the country's youth calling loudly for him to resume his duties as Libya's leader. Needless to say, he eventually bowed to the "popular will."

The Revolutionary Command Council was not pleased to have him back, but in light of his immense popularity and control of the nation's few political institutions, there was little the RCC could do. On April 6, 1974, they made their feelings known by announcing that Brother Colonel was being relieved of his day-to-day duties so that he might "devote himself to theoretical and ideological work to bolster the march of the revolution." In other words, they meant to give him a sinecure — an ostensibly high position that offered little actual power. He was to be replaced by Major Abdel Salem Jalloud, who had long been his trustworthy second-in-command.

Jalloud, however, could not disregard the public outcry that Qaddafi stirred up in his own behalf. He quickly announced that he would "share power"

Qaddafi has failed to command leadership in pan-Arab affairs because, among other things, he brooks no softening of his blend of strict orthodox Islam and radical socialism.
—from a report issued by the Congressional Quarterly Inc.

AP/WIDE WORLD PHOTOS

Automobiles lining up to buy gasoline clog a Manhattan avenue in early 1974. At the time, the United States faced a severe gasoline shortage due, at least in part, to the five-month oil embargo imposed by Arab nations, including Libya, during the Yom Kippur War.

with Qaddafi, who would remain in charge of the military — the key to ruling Libya. Qaddafi also retained his positions as chairman of the RCC and president of the ASU. When the dust settled, Qaddafi's power and stature were pretty much as they had been before the Council tried to throw him out. Most observers agreed that there had been little real chance of Qaddafi being forced to relinquish power.

AP/WIDE WORLD PHOTOS

Making a flurry of trips between Moscow, Tel Aviv, Cairo, and Washington, U.S. Secretary of State Henry Kissinger helped to negotiate an end, on November 11, 1973, to the Yom Kippur War. In further rounds of "shuttle diplomacy," he would secure troop removals and engineer the 1975 Sinai agreement, which called for partial Israeli withdrawal from the Sinai peninsula.

If Qaddafi had not been distracted, the Revolutionary Command Council might never have been able to act against him in the first place. For six months Brother Colonel's attention had not been on Libya, but on Egypt and the ever-present thorn in his side, Anwar Sadat. He had been preoccupied with foreign affairs, starting with the sudden eruption of the Yom Kippur War.

In 1973 Yom Kippur, the most sacred Jewish holy day, fell on Saturday, October 6. Early that morning the Egyptians crossed the Suez Canal and mounted a surprise attack against Israel. Syrian troops simultaneously attacked Israeli forces stationed in the Golan Heights.

Although Qaddafi had earlier supplied Egypt's armed forces with a great deal of materiel for future strikes against Israel — including two squadrons of Mirage jets and an armored brigade — and joined with other Arab nations in an oil embargo against Israel's allies, he was resentful of being excluded from Assad and Sadat's strategic planning of the war. He was also suspicious of the fact that Sadat, whom Qaddafi believed had long been willing to compromise with Israel, had suddenly decided upon anti-Zionist action. Qaddafi did not believe that Sadat was actually committed to the annihilation of Israel.

Apparent evidence of Sadat's lack of commitment emerged early in the war. The Israelis were overwhelmed by the initial Egyptian attack and retreated in confusion. Then the Egyptians used new Russian missiles to shatter a counterattack by the Israeli air force. They quickly advanced 10 miles into Israeli territory. And then, inexplicably, with no resistance to speak of in front of them, the Egyptian army halted. The order to do so came from Sadat.

Why? Qaddafi thought he knew. He issued a statement that Sadat "lacked the guts to wage war."

In fact, Sadat had launched the war at least in part to force the Israelis to sit down at the bargaining table with Egypt, and he had called the halt as an act of good faith. Sadat based his strategy on the theory that military victory over Israel was impossible because at the last minute of any conflict the United States would always come to the rescue of the tiny nation. (Indeed, President Richard M. Nixon had ordered a worldwide U.S. military alert at the beginning of the Yom Kippur War, and the U.S. Sixth Fleet had converged on the Mediterranean Sea.)

Qaddafi's criticism became even more bitter when Egypt and Israel sat down at the peace table. He called the war a "betrayal" and said that from the start it had been nothing but a trick designed by Sadat to give him an excuse to surrender to the Israelis. When the price of oil rose because of the embargo against Israel's allies imposed by the other Arab countries, Qaddafi said that greed for profits had been the real reason for the war all along. Finally he accused Sadat of having made a deal with Washington to start the Yom Kippur War to distract American attention from the growing Watergate scandal and enable President Nixon to maintain his office.

Sadat, whose style was always very different from Qaddafi's, did not dignify the Libyan's absurd charges with a response. Instead, he made the deeply symbolic gesture of inviting Libya's deposed king, Idris I, to live in Cairo, where he was immediately granted Egyptian citizenship. The Arab world understood that Sadat intended the action as a deep insult to Qaddafi.

It was too much. Though an earlier coup attempt against Sadat sponsored by Qaddafi had failed, Brother Colonel put up a great deal of Libyan oil money to try again.

Again the attempt was unsuccessful. The failure this time was most embarrassing to Qaddafi. Sadat exposed the plot and produced evidence proving Brother Colonel's role in financing it. He did not

AP/WIDE WORLD PHOTOS

Soviet Premier Alexei Kosygin, with whom in May 1975 Qaddafi concluded a major arms deal, estimated at $1 billion. In spite of this agreement, Qaddafi continued to denigrate both superpowers as "imperialists," insisting that he could not differentiate between the two "K's" — Kosygin and Kissinger.

I am not a communist, but I might be obliged—just to nag America—to become a communist out of spite.
—MUAMMAR EL-QADDAFI

even have to denounce Qaddafi himself. All of the other heads of Arab states understandably took a dim view of an Arab leader interfering in the internal affairs of another Islamic state and condemned Qaddafi for his actions.

Indeed, Qaddafi's hostile plots against Sadat made him very unpopular in the Arab world. If he would act against Sadat, what fellow Arab ruler would he not act against? Hence it was no surprise that when Faisal, the king of Saudi Arabia, was murdered on March 25, 1975, Qaddafi, who had criticized Faisal for not supporting the Palestinians strongly enough, was suspected of ordering the killing.

He was in fact innocent of this act. The killing was not political, but rather the result of a family squabble. Still, the extent to which suspicion fell on Qaddafi is a measure of how much the other Middle Eastern leaders were beginning to distrust him. Three events, one after the other, combined in their minds to heighten their suspicion.

First, in 1973, a Soviet geological survey reported that the Aouzou Strip — a 27,000-square-mile-territory located within Chad along the Libyan border — contained uranium ore and oil. Shortly thereafter, Qaddafi sent in Libyan troops and annexed the area. He has maintained since that the Aouzou Strip is Libyan territory.

Second, after years of anti-Soviet rhetoric that had continued even after the conclusion of the 1971 oil deal, Qaddafi invited Soviet Premier Alexei N. Kosygin to Libya in May 1975. The visit resulted in the granting of a $1-billion Soviet aid package, under which Libya would be able to purchase from the Soviets heavy armaments and manufacturing machinery at low cost. The key element of the deal was that the Soviet Union promised to build Libya an atomic reactor that would be capable of some day producing a nuclear bomb — conceivably fueled with uranium from the Aouzou Strip.

The third event, the one that most upset the Arab world, was a raid on an OPEC meeting in Vienna on December 21, 1975, conducted by the Popular Revolutionary Front for the Liberation of Palestine

(PRFLP). Members of the PRFLP, a militaristic splinter group of the PLO openly sponsored by Qaddafi, attacked the meeting, took the oil ministers hostage, and killed three victims, one of whom was a Libyan OPEC economist.

Most evidence indicates that Qaddafi probably had nothing to do with planning the raid. Nevertheless, he refused to go along with other Arab heads of state in condemning it. In addition, when the PRFLP guerrillas read a declaration over Austrian radio, it contained a statement condemning Sadat as "a traitor to Islam" in inflammatory language that seemed to echo suspiciously Qaddafi's own statements about the Egyptian president. When the terrorists finally swapped their hostages for an Austrian plane, which they flew to Libya, Qaddafi welcomed them as a legitimate "arm of the Arab revolution" despite their having murdered one of his own government emissaries.

Even the Libyan people were taken aback. What kind of ruler was it, they asked themselves, who valued renegades — denounced even by the PLO — over one of his own people? Was Qaddafi's real loyalty to Libya, they wondered, or to Arab terrorism?

A map of the Organization of Petroleum Exporting Countries (OPEC). During the 1970s, the 13-nation oil cartel implemented a series of price hikes that raised havoc with Western economies. Qaddafi's continual deviations from OPEC supply agreements infuriated fellow members, as did his refusal to condemn a December 1975 raid by Palestinian terrorists on an OPEC meeting in Vienna.

AP/WIDE WORLD PHOTOS

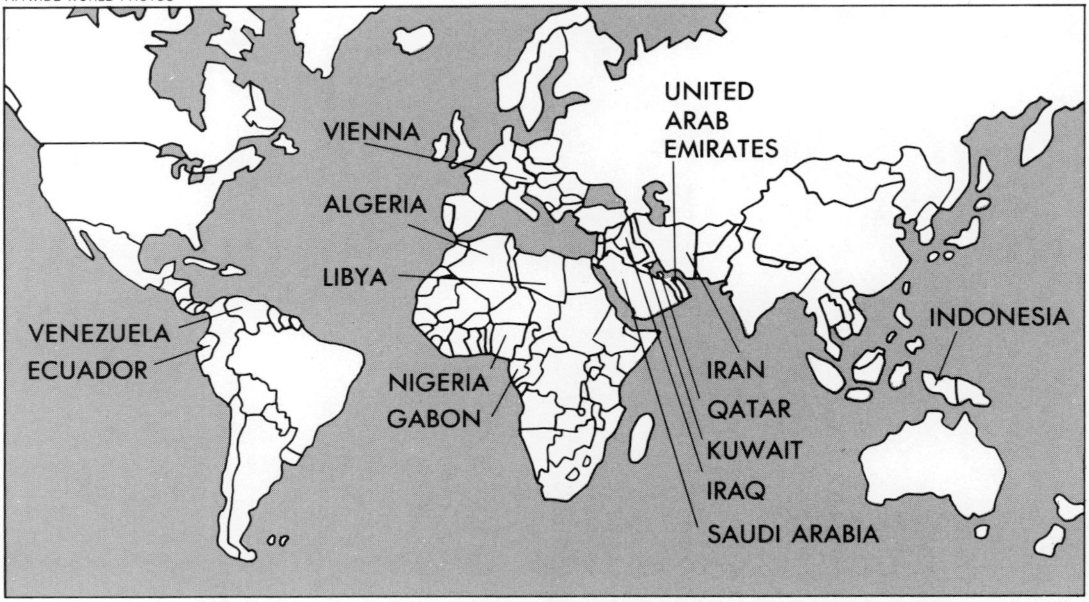

6

Isolation

In March 1976 Qaddafi accused Tunisian President Habib Bourguiba of being "an agent of American colonialism" and dispatched three Libyan commandos to attempt to kill both him and the Tunisian foreign minister. The agents failed, but attempts to destabilize the Tunisian government continued over the next 14 months due to Qaddafi's desire to acquire abundant oil reserves that had been recently discovered on the continental shelf in the Tunisian Gulf of Gabes. It was estimated that 20 million tons of oil could be extracted from the shelf every year.

He has lifted his desert realm out of obscurity, and his people out of poverty and the shadow of underdevelopment. Yet his zeal has turned half the world outside into enemies.
—JOHN K. COOLEY
American journalist, on Qaddafi

On May 27, 1977, Qaddafi abandoned political methods and went after the oil directly. He leased an oil-drilling rig belonging to Reading and Bates, an American company. The government-owned Libyan National Oil Corporation hired American personnel to operate it. The rig was brought into the Gulf of Gabes under escort by the Libyan navy. When Tunisia objected, Qaddafi sent in heavily armed Libyan soldiers by helicopter to protect the American technicians. Tunisia lodged a formal protest with the Arab League, but Qaddafi ignored it and kept on drilling for oil.

Qaddafi was also stirring up trouble in the Sudan. At one time, President Gaafer al-Nimeiry of Sudan had been an ally, but now he was a supporter of Sadat and an ally of the United States.

By 1976 Qaddafi's enigmatic personality had become a key variable in the equation of Libyan politics. To much of the world, he was a detestable archvillain — "100 percent sick and possessed of the devil," as Sadat described him. But to his followers, he was the lone voice of truth.

REUTERS/BETTMANN NEWSPHOTOS

Sadat listens intently to Israeli Prime Minister Menachem Begin during the Egyptian president's historic visit to Jerusalem in November 1977. It was the first time an Arab leader had ever traveled to the Jewish state. The trip led to the March 1979 Camp David peace accords, but also alienated Egypt from hard-line Arab neighbors like Libya.

UPI/BETTMANN NEWSPHOTOS

Returning from a trip there, Nimeiry found his country in the grip of a rebellion led by the Sudanese army. He was greeted at the airport in Khartoum by grenades. Miraculously, Nimeiry survived the attack and, with help from the Egyptian air force, put down the rebellion.

After the Sudanese officers behind the attempted coup confessed that they had been enlisted by Qaddafi, Nimeiry went before the UN Security Council to protest "an act of banditry designed by Libya." A former Sudanese prime minister admitted that he and Qaddafi had planned the action together. Some 97 disloyal officers and 1,000 Sudanese rebel troops had been trained in Libyan camps and equipped with Libyan arms.

Nimeiry signed a joint defense agreement with Sadat. The treaty constituted a warning to Qaddafi that if he meddled in the Sudan again, he would have to contend with Egypt. Sadat was fed up with Qaddafi's aggression. The Egyptian Intelligence Service had learned that Brother Colonel had plans to "attack Arab presidents, hijack aircraft and storm embassies." There was a "Qaddafi hit-list" headed by the name Anwar Sadat.

Libyan-Egyptian tensions mounted. On July 12, 1977, four heavily armed Libyan saboteurs were caught crossing the Egyptian border. A few days later Libyan soldiers fired across the border and killed an Egyptian civilian. Then a Libyan army unit crossed the boundary, killed 10 Egyptian soldiers, and took 33 others captive. When the Egyptians hit back by bombing military bases in Libya, there was no longer any doubt. It was war!

. . . a split personality — both evil.

—GAAFER AL-NIMEIRY
former president of Sudan,
on Qaddafi

From the beginning, Egypt displayed superior strength. In the first actual battle, waged on July 21, Libya suffered heavy casualties. The Egyptians captured 40 of their tanks and 30 other armored vehicles. On July 24 the powerful Egyptian air force destroyed Libya's El Adem air base and two radar stations essential to Libya's air defense. Following this attack, Egyptian ground troops began advancing rapidly into Libya.

The other Middle Eastern nations were disgusted by the spectacle of two Arab countries at each other's throats. It was this that saved Qaddafi. They pressured Sadat into a cease-fire. He and Qaddafi agreed to arbitrate their differences.

They continued, however, to attack each other verbally. Qaddafi accused Sadat of invading Libya on orders from the United States and Israel. Sadat responded by calling Qaddafi "the lunatic of Libya" whose overthrow would "benefit not only the Arab people, but the whole world."

Despite this exchange of insults, the two sides were able to agree on August 28 to pull their troops back to the previous border. The rhetoric cooled. Indeed, on October 7, Qaddafi called the war a "catastrophe" in a speech he made in Tripoli and went on to say that he would put the Libyan army under Egyptian command if Sadat would mount an attack to "liberate Sinai from the Zionist enemy."

But instead of launching such an attack, Sadat went to Israel a month later, on November 19, 1977, and sat down with Israeli Prime Minister Menachem Begin to discuss peace between their two countries. It was the first official visit by an Arab leader to the state of Israel. To Qaddafi, this was the ultimate betrayal. He had the General People's Congress issue a proclamation branding Sadat's meeting with Begin "a crime against the entire Arab nation."

Qaddafi's "Arab nation" was surprisingly inclusive. Turning his attention from East to West, Brother Colonel announced that "the Red Indians of America are of Libyan origin!" This did not, however, apply to young American Indians who joined the Boy Scouts. The Boy Scouts, he charged, were a front for the CIA.

Outlandish claims like these reinforced the widespread international perception of Qaddafi as a paranoid eccentric. His attention wandered, he was irritable, and his reactions were increasingly inappropriate. He was harsh and unyielding to those who dared to challenge his assumptions. He developed a painful and serious stomach condition that Libyan doctors were unable to diagnose or treat. English physicians were flown in for consultation, but their efforts proved fruitless. To those who knew him in private, Qaddafi seemed to be falling apart.

Qaddafi with his wife and four of their seven children in the family tent at the Bab al-Azzizia barracks. The Libyan leader displayed the trappings of Bedouin culture in order to establish himself as a man of the people.

UPI/BETTMANN NEWSPHOTOS

Increasingly paranoid, Qaddafi stopped trusting his bodyguards. He replaced them with members of his own Berber tribe, whose loyalty, he felt, would be unmitigated because of the blood relation. At the same time, he strengthened security at his headquarters in the Bab al-Azzizia barracks. He installed the most sophisticated missile-launching antiaircraft and artillery weapons to protect the compound against both land and air attacks.

There was justification for Qaddafi's fears. Three major coup attempts occurred between January 1978 and mid-1981. All three were organized by high-placed Libyan government officials who had seemed to be very close to Qaddafi.

What you view as terrorism is the Palestinian struggle for liberation against the Israelis.
—MUAMMAR EL-QADDAFI

Captain Mohammed Idris Sharif, the chief of Libyan military intelligence, organized the first conspiracy, under the auspices of the CIA. His aim was to assassinate Qaddafi and to kill all high-ranking government officials known to be loyal to him. But the plot was infiltrated by Qaddafi's agents. Colonel Sharif and several other plotters were arrested, although not all of them were caught immediately. On March 6, 1978, saboteurs blew up a helicopter that had been scheduled to transport Qaddafi, killing 11 people. Only a last minute change of plans saved his life. More Libyan officers were arrested and sent to join Colonel Sharif in his primitive desert prison.

There was another attempt to overthrow Qaddafi, in August 1980. Driss Chehaibi, who commanded the Tobruk garrison and was an old and trusted friend of Qaddafi's, was behind it. He confessed to having been put up to the plot by agents of the French government. Like the previous coup, this one also failed, and the plotters were imprisoned.

On May 22, 1981, a third coup was mounted. This one involved El-Magarha tribesmen from the Fezzan district of Libya. Former Major — now Colonel — Abdel Salem Jalloud, who had once shared power with Qaddafi but had now dropped back to second-in-command, was a member of the El-Magarha tribe.

The plot was aborted. Despite Qaddafi's suspicions, it was never proved that Colonel Jalloud had been involved. Qaddafi did not investigate the matter for fear Jalloud might mobilize his strong power base against Brother Colonel. The Libyan leader was more concerned with evidence showing that the Egyptians were behind this attempt.

> **The Green Book, *Qaddafi seems to feel, has provided the main script for his own role as the lonely superstar of modern history.***
>
> —JOHN K. COOLEY
> American journalist

There had been three attempted coups, each one involving a powerful enemy. Qaddafi had become more than just unpopular; from the nature of the American, French, and Egyptian reactions, it was obvious that his constant interference in the affairs of other statesmen was considered a threat to world security. Meanwhile, there was an increasing number of protests and demonstrations against him by his own countrymen.

There had been signs of discontent as early as January 1976. At that time, he had attempted to curb opposition to his regime by stifling the activities of intellectuals, who were thought to be more prone to dissent, but at the same time he had enacted measures to improve the Libyan educational system. Educated youth naturally ended up opposing Qaddafi's anti-intellectual policies. When the people's committees tried to impose government control over student unions at secondary schools and colleges, the students rebelled.

A protest demonstration in Benghazi turned into a riot. Police moved in to break it up. Rocks were thrown and shooting broke out. When the smoke cleared, 10 students had been killed and dozens more were wounded.

Insensitive to the damage the incident had done to his popularity, Qaddafi soon thereafter carried out a series of purge trials that lasted through April 1977. Ten government officials were sentenced to prison for life. Twenty-three Libyan army officers were sentenced to death for "treacherous activities." Four had belonged to Qaddafi's original Revolutionary Command Council; they escaped the country before their sentences could be carried out. Qaddafi denounced them as "traitors to the homeland." The 19 others were publicly hanged. Officers who had served with them were ordered to be present at the executions in order to—in Qaddafi's words—"teach them a lesson."

The purge only fueled opposition to Brother Colonel. By 1980, demonstrations and riots were commonplace occurrences in Tripoli, Benghazi, and Tobruk.

Some groups took more drastic measures. One anti-Qaddafi group destroyed three highly productive oil wells. They threatened to blow up others unless Qaddafi resigned. Some 100,000 Libyans, most of them among the country's well-educated citizens, fled to other lands. Three thousand others were prevented from leaving when Qaddafi had them arrested and jailed for expressing "incorrect" social views.

AP/WIDE WORLD PHOTOS

Tripoli youths demonstrate against Egypt on December 4, 1977, two days after Syria, Iraq, Libya, Algeria, and South Yemen had met in that city to declare a "new front for resistance and opposition" to Sadat's peace initiatives. Egypt promptly severed diplomatic relations with the five countries.

Abdel Salem Jalloud was suspected of involvement in the El-Magarha tribe's aborted 1981 plot against Qaddafi — which, along with two failed army conspiracies, convinced the Libyan leader to bolster his security forces. His massive bodyguard included East Germans, members of his own Berber tribe, and an elite squad of women soldiers.

UPI/BETTMANN NEWSPHOTOS

Qaddafi tried to hold onto his popularity by calling attention to his simple Bedouin image. Periodically, he summoned journalists to his goatskin tent in the Bab al-Azzizia barracks to interview him.

Always he called their attention to the tent's traditional Berber patchwork roof. He pointed out the tribal embroidery adorning the tent poles. He posed for pictures astride the animal skin rugs on the floor of sand. He played the part of the simple desert Arab to the hilt.

But many journalists saw through the facade. They noted other things, like the expensive antique English leather chair. They observed the handsomely carved and shellacked imported coffee table. They spied the stereo and the pile of cassettes, the embroidered silk pajamas crumpled up beside his cot, and the carton of cigarettes — forbidden by Islamic law—beside the pail of goat's milk.

Nevertheless, Qaddafi was not all sham. There

truly were some beliefs from his desert background that he still valued. He believed in the closeness of family, and he understood that this closeness could make a person vulnerable. This was doubtless in Qaddafi's mind when, in early 1978, Libya's ambassador in Washington informed him that Billy Carter, the brother of American President Jimmy Carter, wanted to visit Tripoli to talk about oil. The ambassador told Qaddafi that Billy had asked for and received a briefing on Libya from two members of the U.S. National Security Council. Sensing an opportunity to embarrass the president, Qaddafi gave permission for the visit.

Billy came to Tripoli in September 1978. He stayed seven days, attending banquets in his honor and receiving the most lavish treatment. The Libyan government paid the entire cost of the visit, and

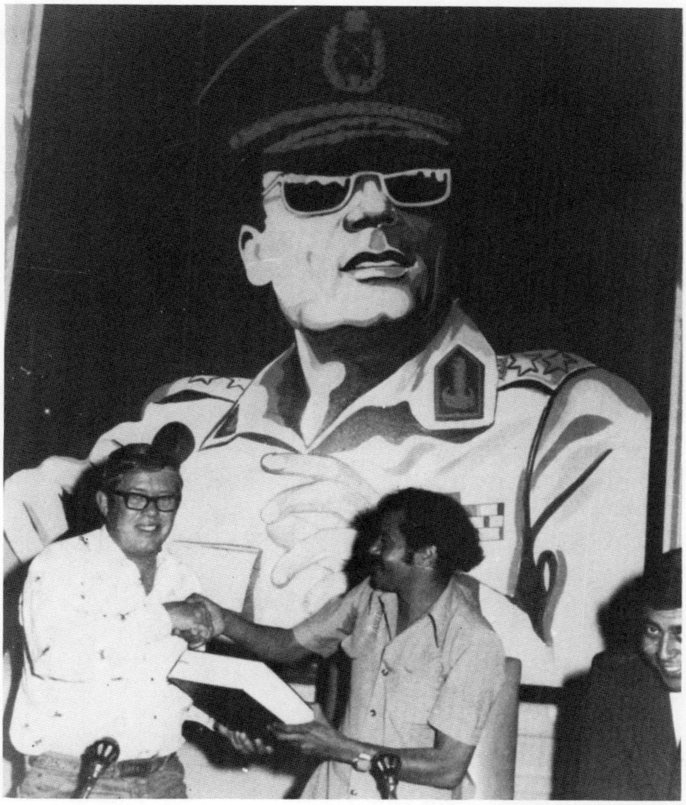

AP/WIDE WORLD PHOTOS

On the first of several trips to Libya, Billy Carter, brother of U.S. President Jimmy Carter, poses under an enormous painting of Qaddafi. Billy's extensive dealings with Libya, including his receipt of a $220,000 loan, prompted government investigations that greatly embarrassed his brother during the 1980 presidential campaign.

Ronald Reagan accepts the Republican presidential nomination in July 1980. As president of the United States, Reagan adopted a much tougher attitude toward Libya than had his predecessor, Jimmy Carter. Singling out Qaddafi as a major supporter of international terrorism and a Soviet surrogate, Reagan closed the Libyan Embassy in Washington in May 1981.

Qaddafi's underlings made sure that foreign journalists took pictures of Billy Carter being driven by a chauffeur in a Libyan government limousine.

In February 1979 Billy reciprocated Qaddafi's hospitality by inviting a Libyan trade delegation to Plains, Georgia, the president's hometown. Billy personally escorted them through the Carter family's peanut processing plant. Qaddafi was not displeased when Billy Carter condemned "the Jewish media tearing up the Arab countries" and noted that the world had "a hell of a lot more Arabians than Jews."

> ***I find he's not only a barbarian, but he's flaky.***
>
> —RONALD REAGAN
> American president,
> on Qaddafi

Billy made a deal with the Charter Oil Company of Florida in August 1979. He would be paid 55 cents for every barrel of oil he could obtain from Libya in addition to the crude that Charter was already importing. Realizing that he might make millions of dollars from this deal, Billy went back to Libya and asked to meet with Qaddafi.

UPI/BETTMANN NEWSPHOTOS

By 1977 Qaddafi's people's revolution had brought major changes to Libya's political and economic structures. Authority at the local level had been transferred to people's committees, each of which administered basic services like housing and education and supplied delegates to the national legislature, the General People's Congress. Ownership of factories had been passed to workers' committees.

We will impose sovereignty on the Gulf of Sidra with our blood!
—MUAMMAR EL-QADDAFI

In Qaddafi's mind, to humiliate Billy was to humiliate his brother, the president of the United States. He kept Billy waiting four weeks for a meeting that never took place. Nevertheless, the Libyans gave Billy additional oil for Charter. Thus Qaddafi passed up neither the opportunity of humiliating the president's brother nor of compromising him.

Brother Colonel was able to compromise him further when Billy, very short of cash, asked his Libyan contacts for money in exchange for providing certain public relations services for the Libyan government. Qaddafi gladly gave it to him. In early 1980 — an election year — Billy received two checks from the Libyans totaling $220,000. Qaddafi authorized a government statement saying that it was a "loan" granted because the Libyans felt Billy might have suffered unfairly because of his association with their country.

When the "loan" came to light, both Congress and the Justice Department investigated. On July 14, 1980, Billy registered with the Justice Department as a Libyan agent, thereby avoiding prosecution. There was a public outcry against a deal having been struck. Because of Qaddafi's use of his brother, President Carter was seriously embarrassed just four months prior to the November 1980 presidential election.

He lost the election to Ronald Reagan. Under Reagan, the United States assumed a much more confrontational stance toward Libya than it had under his predecessor. From the beginning of his first term, Reagan singled out Libya as a major sponsor of international terrorism and targeted Qaddafi's country for an array of coercive measures. In May 1981 all Libyan diplomats were expelled from the United States and the Libyan Embassy in Washington, D.C., was closed. The Reagan administration also provided generous aid to neighboring Arab countries that opposed Qaddafi's rule. Discussions were held with European and Arab countries about the possibility of military action or an oil boycott against Libya. Secretary of State Alexander M. Haig referred privately to Qaddafi as a "cancer" that had to be removed.

In August 1981 Reagan decided to challenge Libya's frequent claim to the Gulf of Sidra, a body of water in the southern Mediterranean, most of which lies more than 12 miles — the international boundary for territorial waters — off the Libyan coast. Insisting that Libya's waters in fact extended 200 miles off the coast, Qaddafi had begun calling the edge of the gulf "the line of death," charging that any country that violated the line would be attacked. On August 19, the U.S. aircraft carrier *Nimitz* led several American ships into the gulf, ostensibly to assert the right of free passage in international waters.

Qaddafi ordered his warplanes into the air to enforce his arbitrary claim to the gulf waters. Two of them were shot down by U.S. Navy F-14 Tomcat fighters after supposedly attacking the American aircraft. For the first time the two countries had squared off in battle. It would not be the last time.

The West is mad! It's still with the spirit of the Crusades. They would like to enable the Israelis to control the Arab world, and they want to destroy the Arabs.
—MUAMMAR EL-QADDAFI

Libyans scream anti-American slogans at a rally in Tripoli. Libyan-American tensions came to a head in August 1981 in an air battle over the Mediterranean. U.S. Navy jets shot down two Libyan warplanes that had reportedly attacked American ships on maneuvers in the Gulf of Sidra.

UPI/BETTMANN NEWSPHOTOS

7

Terror and Revenge

> *Colonel Muammar Qaddafi of Libya has stomped across the world's stage as our most dramatic, most photogenic, most hissable arch-villain.*
>
> —DOYLE MCMANUS
> American journalist

Though most Arab countries officially objected to the American military strike in the Gulf of Sidra, many of them privately applauded the action. By 1981 Qaddafi's religious quest for Arab unity had alienated most of the Arab leaders whose approval he so ardently sought. His exaggerated perception of Libya as a world power, his virulent hatred of Israel, and his constant meddling in the affairs of neighboring states, particularly his support of insurgents in Chad, Tunisia, Morocco, Ethiopia, and the Sudan, had repelled even hard-line Arab states. In 1974 Qaddafi had reportedly said that "he would arm and train revolutionaries to overthrow the governments of Tunisia, Egypt, and Algeria if Arab unity could not be achieved by 'normal means,' " according to the 1981 Congressional Quarterly book entitled *The Middle East*. By 1981 every Arab leader was forced to wonder whether he was next on Qaddafi's hit list.

Then, on October 6, 1981, less than two months after the Gulf of Sidra confrontation, Egyptian President Anwar Sadat was assassinated. He had been watching a military parade commemorating the 1973 Arab-Israeli war when a jeep had suddenly pulled out of the parade line and its occupants had strafed the reviewing stand with automatic fire. There was immediate speculation that Qaddafi had engineered the killing. Suspicion increased when Saad al-Shazly, an Egyptian exile with strong ties

Libyan children brandish Soviet-made rifles while riding atop a hearse carrying victims of a massive American air attack on Tripoli and Benghazi on April 15, 1986. The raid, conducted by more than 150 U.S. Air Force and Navy jets, came in response to Libya's alleged role in a terrorist bombing of a West German nightclub.

UPI/BETTMANN NEWSPHOTOS

to Qaddafi, claimed responsibility for the attack. Shazly had been a powerful figure in the Nasser administration, but he had lost favor with Sadat during the short-lived period of the Federation of Arab Republics. As a general in command of combined Egyptian-Libyan forces in Tripoli, he had constantly taken Qaddafi's side in the frequent disputes between the two nations. His apparent bias toward Libya and his alleged role in an earlier plot against Sadat finally led to his arrest. He then escaped to Algeria, where he allegedly planned the conspiracy against Sadat.

The Egyptian government's official position, however, was that Sadat's killers were an isolated group of Muslim extremists who had acted without outside help. Even though Qaddafi was probably not directly involved in the assassination, he was certainly overjoyed with the result. To Qaddafi, Sadat's death rid the Arab world of its foremost traitor, the man who had stood in the way of Arab unity and who had negotiated peace with the ultimate enemy, Israel. Libya was the first country to issue an official reaction to the attack. A commentator on Tripoli

Soldiers remove the body of one of the four men who assassinated Egyptian President Anwar Sadat as he reviewed a military parade on October 6, 1981. Though Egypt said the killers were independent Muslim fanatics, Qaddafi claimed credit for the shooting. Libya's Tripoli Radio hailed it as "a victory for the Arabs against treachery."

UPI/BETTMANN NEWSPHOTOS

Radio interrupted regular programming to say, "International news agencies have just announced the greatest news about a victory for the Arabs and Egyptians against treachery." The announcer went on to call Sadat "Anwar the tyrant and slaughterer."

In dealing with opposition to his government, Qaddafi himself had become a slaughterer, not hesitating to use Libyans or hired foreigners to eliminate enemies at home or abroad. In February 1980 Libyan revolutionary committees issued a decree authorizing the "physical liquidation" of enemies of the revolution. During the first three months after the decree, 10 Libyan exiles who opposed Qaddafi were assassinated in Europe; these 10 were "mostly people of modest station who played no important role in the Libyan political opposition," according to John K. Cooley, an American writer. On April 28, 1980, after Amnesty International — a group that monitors human rights abuses worldwide — had condemned the murders, the official Libyan newspaper *Al-Azhaf al-Akhdar* (*The Green Road*) ran articles celebrating the "liquidation program" and warning that Libyans who failed to heed decrees asking them to return from abroad were jeopardizing their families.

The trappings of Qaddafi's visionary dreams — the flags, slogans, pictures of him, and other revolutionary paraphernalia that suggest the bleakness of Orwell's* 1984, *transferred by magic to the coasts of Africa — are everywhere.

—JOHN K. COOLEY
American journalist

One victim was Ezzeddin Ghadamsi, who had been Libya's ambassador to Austria until he was fired for publicly disagreeing with Libyan government policies. When after his dismissal he continued to speak out against the Qaddafi regime, a Libyan hit-team went to Vienna and shot him. Despite being gravely wounded, Ghadamsi survived the attack. Ahmed Barrani, a 35-year-old opponent of Qaddafi who had left Libya to seek refuge in Cyprus, was less lucky. Bullets fired by Qaddafi-hired assassins killed him. A particularly gruesome example of Qaddafi's ruthlessness took place when former Qaddafi government official Omar Mekeshi, who had fled to Morocco, was returned to Libyan jurisdiction. At Qaddafi's urging, the people's committees organized a reception for Mekeshi at the Tripoli airport. As he came off the plane, he was seized and stomped to death on the runway.

Meanwhile, Qaddafi continued to rankle American officials by supporting radical groups within the United States. In February 1981 Qaddafi established ties with Louis Farrakhan's Nation of Islam, a religious political organization founded by black Muslims. Farrakhan would later become infamous throughout the United States for his anti-Semitic remarks. His organization, though it preached a radical message of black separatism, had managed to attract a surprisingly large following. In a 1981 closed circuit radio broadcast from Tripoli to the Chicago branch of the Nation of Islam, Qaddafi called for a rebellion inside the United States. Blacks in the American military, Qaddafi said, should rise up against their officers. He promised to train and arm those who would desert. Though Farrakhan turned down this offer, he did accept 5 million dollars from Qaddafi. He later insisted that the money was "simply a loan to be repaid," but it was in fact a loan without interest. The U.S. State Department warned that the Nation of Islam was "a front group for Libyan terrorists."

The latest age of slavery is the white race's enslavement of the black race. The black man will not forget until he has achieved rehabilitation.
—MUAMMAR EL-QADDAFI

The State Department was also upset by Libya's increasing military involvement in Chad. In the late 1970s Qaddafi had supported Muslim rebels led by Goukouni Oueddei with money, arms, and Libyan soldiers. The confusing Chad war dragged on for years. In 1980–1981 Libya had sent thousands of troops into Chad at the request of Goukouni, now the nation's president, in an attempt to keep him in power. Although the Libyan troops scored a major victory in 1981 when they overran the Chadian capital city of N'Djamena, Qaddafi insisted, "We have not interfered in Chad and are not occupying Chad. Our role is merely in keeping the peace."

France, for one, did not believe Qaddafi's claims that Libya played no part in the Chadian civil war and that the conflict was strictly the result of an internal problem. After Hissène Habré, who was backed by the U.S. and France, overthrew Goukouni in 1982, Qaddafi funded Goukouni's counterrevolution. In August 1983 Libyan aircraft helped Goukouni's troops to capture strategic townships in northern Chad, prompting Habré to request the assistance of French troops.

When France installed 3,000 heavily armed troops in August 1983, Qaddafi responded that he was only taking necessary action to protect the Chadian people from "genocide" by CIA-backed French "colonial forces." While at first the French troops did nothing more than stare at their Libyan counterparts across a defensive line, by early 1984 the two nations were directly engaged. By April Libya was reported to have annexed the northern desert region of Chad and to have 6,000 troops in the region.

During the early 1980s, in accordance with Qaddafi's political and social revolution inside Libya, he began to convert Libyan embassies to "People's Bureaus." Experienced foreign service officers were replaced by zealots chosen by people's committees. In Great Britain, the people's committees ousted the entire staff of Libya's embassy. The building in London's St. James Square was taken over by inexperienced Qaddafi loyalists. Trying to find out who was in charge, or at least who had the authority to conduct business for the Libyan government, proved impossible for the British Foreign Office.

On April 17, 1984, the People's Bureau in St. James Square was picketed by two opposing Libyan groups, one protesting the British government's recent arrest of alleged Arab terrorists, and the other—which included a number of political exiles—demonstrating against Qaddafi's tyranny. When the two groups clashed, London police acted to separate them. As they were doing so, a stone was thrown at the embassy building and fell short. Nevertheless, shots were fired from the building in response. Eleven people were hit. One of them was killed instantly. The dead victim was Constable Yvonne Fletcher of the London police.

Most of the world was outraged. Many governments issued statements demanding that those who had fired the bullets from inside the Libyan embassy building be punished. But Qaddafi refused to allow British investigators inside the People's Bureau, claiming diplomatic immunity. Eleven days

UPI/BETTMANN NEWSPHOTOS

By 1981 Qaddafi's response to dissent had become extremely harsh. His agents abroad had assassinated several exiled Libyans following a February 1980 government decree urging "physical liquidation" of enemies of the revolution. At home, hundreds of dissidents reportedly had been rounded up, tortured, and interned indefinitely.

after Constable Fletcher's murder, the British decided to expel the entire staff of the embassy. The Libyans were escorted out and permitted to fly back to Libya. Behind them they left an arsenal of weapons and dozens of empty shell casings from the ammunition that had taken Constable Fletcher's life. Thereafter, all Libyans with connections to the Qaddafi government were forced to leave England, including all representatives of the Libyan oil industry — resulting in serious damage to Libya's economy. In retaliation Qaddafi arrested six British citizens living in Libya and would not allow them to consult with British government representatives — a direct violation of international law. Two of them remained in jail for over 10 months, though neither was charged with any crime.

Quite clearly Qaddafi has played a major role in terrorism, but he by no means exercises control over the myriad Middle East groups who target the U.S. and the West for a variety of reasons. Qaddafi may have a 'go' switch for some terrorist groups, but not a 'stop' switch.

—BRIAN JENKINS
Rand Corporation expert on terrorism

The embassy shootout fanned the fire of growing domestic discontent. On March 25, 1984, a government munitions warehouse in Benghazi had been blown up, killing 200 people. Right after the embassy shootout in London, the auditorium of a university in Tripoli was burned down in an anti-Qaddafi protest. Arsonists also torched a government-run supermarket. In May the National Salvation Front was formed by freedom fighters opposed to Qaddafi. The Front received some funding and training from the CIA. They raided an army storehouse outside Tripoli and seized a sizable number of rocket-launchers and machine guns. On May 8 they attacked the Bab al-Azzizia barracks. A battle raged between them and Qaddafi's bodyguard for over five hours. When the bodyguard was reinforced by army troops from outside the barracks, the rebels were forced to withdraw without having achieved their objective of assassinating Qaddafi.

In August 1985 there was further indication that Qaddafi's hold on Libya was becoming tenuous. During that month he had moved some 25,000 Libyan army troops to the Tunisian border with the intention of mounting a full-scale invasion. When the order came to begin the attack, key units of the Libyan army mutinied. Later, Qaddafi would deny having given the order.

In the meantime, the United States had imposed further political and economic sanctions on Qaddafi in response to his continued attempts to destabilize African and Arab regimes and to his taunts and public threats against Americans. In March 1982 the United States banned all imports of Libyan oil. At the same time, military deliveries to two of Qaddafi's neighbors, Egypt and the Sudan, were sped up. American officials were especially concerned about Qaddafi's role as — in the words of British journalist Claire Sterling — "the Daddy Warbucks of world terrorism." By the 1980s Qaddafi had dropped a number of the causes less important to him: the IRA in Northern Ireland, the Basque separatist movement in Spain, and the Muslim rebels in the Philippines. But he had continued to provide money, training, equipment, and sanctuary to the PLO and its various guerrilla groups. Thus, he became a major focus of extensive American efforts under Reagan to combat terrorism in all its manifestations. Under the "Shultz Doctrine" — named after George Shultz, who had replaced Haig as secretary of state in 1982 — several officials in the Reagan administration urged the president to retaliate militarily against known sources of terrorist violence. Other Reagan aides opposed this option because, they argued, it was difficult in most cases to identify the perpetrators. It was especially hard to produce incontrovertible evidence proving that national leaders had engineered attacks. Any retaliatory strike against another sovereign state also ran the risk of killing innocent civilians and producing a larger conflict.

UPI/BETTMANN NEWSPHOTOS

Louis Farrakhan, the leader of the Nation of Islam, a radical group of black American Muslims. Notorious for his frequent anti-Semitic remarks and his threats against mainstream black politicians, Farrakhan rejected Qaddafi's 1985 offer to supply his group with military aid and training.

Qaddafi was not the only leader against whom the United States contemplated action. Iran and Syria were thought to be behind several terrorist attacks, including bombings in Lebanon that killed almost 250 Americans in 1983 and 1984. But to American leaders, Qaddafi was the most attractive target. Not only was he the most vocal supporter of terrorism, he was also the weakest militarily and the most isolated diplomatically.

In 1985 a dramatic rise in terrorist acts commit-

> *If Abu Nidal is a terrorist, then so is George Washington.*
> —MUAMMAR EL-QADDAFI

ted by Arab groups against European and American targets increased pressure on Reagan — from within his administration and from the American people — to retaliate. On July 22, 1985, an explosion destroyed the offices of Northwest Orient — an American airline — in Copenhagen, Denmark. Simultaneously, a Jewish synagogue and a nursing home in that city were struck by a second bomb. Fourteen people were injured in the two blasts — seven seriously. Islamic Jihad, the group that took credit for the two explosions, had ties to both Qaddafi and Iran. On September 16, 40 people were hurt when members of a terrorist organization led by Abu Nidal set off a Russian grenade in a café in Rome. The café, only 100 yards from the United States Embassy, was well known to be frequented by Americans.

Next came the *Achille Lauro* incident. On October 7, members of the PLO seized the Italian cruise ship *Achille Lauro* in Egyptian waters and held 400 passengers and the crew hostage. They demanded the release of 50 Palestinian guerrillas being held in Israel. While negotiations proceeded, the terrorists murdered Leon Klinghoffer, an American who had previously suffered a stroke and was confined to a wheelchair. They shot him in the head and threw his body overboard.

When Mohammed Abu Abbas, the PLO leader who admitted having authorized the seizure of the cruise ship but not the murder of Klinghoffer, was subsequently released by both Egyptian and Italian authorities, he fled to Libya. Qaddafi received him with open arms.

AP/WIDE WORLD PHOTOS

Chadians are instructed in the use of artillery by one of 3,000 French troops sent to Chad in August 1983. Chadian President Hissène Habré requested the assistance to help fight the Libyan-supported rebellion of ex-president Goukouni Oueddei.

In the press and to his adversaries, he has appeared as a Darth Vader of the desert, relentlessly plotting global havoc.
—DOYLE MCMANUS
American journalist, on Qaddafi

On November 23, members of the Palestinian terrorist group led by Abu Nidal hijacked an Egyptian airliner bound from Athens to Cairo. During the flight, they shot five people, killing two, an Israeli and an American. When they landed in Malta, an Egyptian commando group tried to recover the plane. In the ensuing battle, 59 passengers were killed, some by Egyptian bullets, others in fires that resulted when the Arab commandos threw grenades inside the plane's cabin.

On December 27, terrorist squads from the Abu Nidal group entered international airports in Rome and Vienna and proceeded to shoot indiscriminately at holiday tourists gathered around airline ticket counters. They also hurled grenades into the throngs of people. Nineteen people were killed, five of them Americans. In the aftermath of the two raids there was evidence suggesting that Abu Nidal was connected to Libya.

Despite the apparent acceleration in terror, Reagan continued to express caution. He seemed to doubt that the United States could successfully identify and retaliate against the actual perpetrators of terrorist actions — Palestinian, Lebanese, and Syrian commandos. Along with his close aide, Secretary of Defense Caspar Weinberger, Reagan worried that carrying out a military strike against Qaddafi — without tangible evidence of his involvement — would alienate European nations with strong economic ties to Libya. Nevertheless, he was willing to again challenge Qaddafi's claims to the Gulf of Sidra in order to bring about a limited military engagement.

On March 24, 1986, the United States took action. The U.S. Navy sailed into the Gulf of Sidra, which Qaddafi continued to claim was the exclusive domain of Libya. Thirty warships and 200 planes swept across the "line of death" in order, according to American officials, to assert the right of international shippers to use the body of water. In the daylong battle that followed, the Americans sank two Libyan patrol boats and damaged three others. A Libyan radar station in Sirte was twice put out of commission. There were no American casualties.

He harbors terrorists, trains them, supplies them, encourages them. You don't have to be Sherlock Holmes to figure it out.

—GEORGE SHULTZ
U.S. secretary of state,
on Qaddafi

For all his rhetoric, Qaddafi had suffered a major defeat.

Less than a week after the fleet had sailed out of the Gulf of Sidra, a group calling itself Arab Revolutionary Cells planted a bomb on a TWA airliner as revenge for the American naval action. The bomb went off while the plane was over Greece and blew a hole in the passenger plane. One of the four Americans killed was an eight-month-old infant. On April 4, hundreds of people were injured when a terrorist bomb ripped apart La Belle, a disco in West Berlin that was known to be frequented by American soldiers. A Turkish woman died, as did an American soldier. A second American died several months later from injuries incurred in the attack. Many of the victims suffered severe burns over large areas of their bodies.

Reportedly, American intelligence decoded a message sent from Tripoli to the East Berlin Libyan People's Bureau the day after the La Belle bombing. "Mission successfully accomplished. Our hand not detected," was allegedly how the message read. There was now no doubt in many American minds that Qaddafi was responsible for terrorist acts aimed at Americans.

Later doubts would be raised. West German intelligence would produce proof that Syria was responsible, not Libya. The possibility existed that Syria's President Assad had prompted the attack because he wanted the U.S. to take retaliatory action against his rival, Qaddafi.

But to Reagan, the United States finally had the "smoking gun" it needed — solid proof that Libya had supported a terrorist attack. This development, along with several other factors, pushed him toward a more militant stance. Terrorism was clearly on the rise; non-military means of combating terrorism had proven ineffective; and the U.S. capture in October 1985 of the *Achille Lauro* hijackers gave the president added confidence in the ability of American forces. On Sunday, April 13, 1986, Reagan gave the go-ahead for a bombing raid against Tripoli and Benghazi, despite getting approval from only three U.S. allies — Great Britain, Israel, and Canada. Later Reagan would explain, "We tried quiet diplomacy.

We tried public condemnation. We tried economic sanctions. . . . But Qaddafi intensified his terrorist war, sending his agents around the world to murder and maim innocents."

On April 14, Operation El Dorado Canyon, as it was code-named by Pentagon planners, began. It was a complex operation that involved more than 150 aircraft and the launching of 60 tons of bombs. It combined more than 100 planes from aircraft carriers stationed in the Mediterranean with U.S. Air Force F-111 fighter planes that flew to Libya all the way from Lakenheath air base near London. (The F-111's were forced to fly an extra 1,200 nautical miles because Spain and France refused to permit use of their airspace for the raid. The 29 F-111's were refueled four times en route by an accompanying squadron of tanker planes.) The attack began under cover of night at 7 P.M. Eastern Standard Time — perfectly coordinated to appear on broadcasts of network evening news programs. The American jets hit five targets: the military side of the Tripoli International Airport, the Bab al-Azzizia barracks where Qaddafi lives, a Tripoli naval base some-

Marilyn Klinghoffer (third from right) grieves for her husband, Leon, who was shot by Palestinian terrorists during the hijacking of the cruise ship *Achille Lauro*. The PLO commandos were later apprehended when American jets dramatically intercepted an Egyptian plane carrying them to freedom; their leader, however, fled to Libya.

AP/WIDE WORLD PHOTOS

> ***You can run, but you can't hide.***
>
> —RONALD REAGAN
> American president,
> in a message to Qaddafi after
> the 1986 American raid on Libya

times used as a commando school, Benina airfield in Benghazi, and military barracks in Benghazi.

In the eyes of American planners, the raid was enormously successful, causing severe damage to Qaddafi's personal headquarters and destroying at least eight Soviet-built Libyan planes. There were two unintended consequences: the loss of a F-111 with its two-man crew, and unintentional civilian casualties. At least 37 civilians reportedly were killed, including Qaddafi's 18-month-old daughter, Hana. The Libyan leader's two sons, Saif al-Arab, 4, and Hamis, 3, were injured and his wife shell-shocked when bombs blew off the front walls of their living quarters. Qaddafi himself escaped what was at least in part an assassination attempt by hiding underground in a bunker where he often sleeps. George Shultz would later refuse to state categorically that murdering the dictator had been a goal, saying "we did not have a strategy saying we wanted to go after Qaddafi personally."

Though its veiled execution attempt had not succeeded, the Reagan administration publicly hailed

AP/WIDE WORLD PHOTOS

Malta airport authorities survey damage to an Egyptian jet. The day before, November 23, 1985, Egyptian troops had stormed the plane attempting to free it from its hijackers, members of a Palestinian terrorist group led by Abu Nidal. Fifty-nine passengers were killed in crossfire and fiery explosions caused by grenades the desperate hijackers threw inside the cabin.

UPI/BETTMANN NEWSPHOTOS

Safia Qaddafi, Muammar's wife, points out damage to her home at the Bab al-Azzizia barracks caused by the April 1986 U.S. air raid. The planners of the American raid insisted that Qaddafi was not the target. Qaddafi's adopted baby daughter allegedly died in the attack.

the raid as a triumph. In a television address afterward, Reagan asserted that the air strike "will not only diminish Colonel Qaddafi's capacity to export terror, it will provide him with incentives and reasons to alter his criminal behavior." Most Americans seemed to agree. Sixty-six percent of the respondents to a *Time* magazine poll said they thought "Reagan was right in ordering the bombing." Though 84 percent said they thought the raid would increase the likelihood of terrorist attacks on Britain, 56 percent said they thought the Libyan bombing would, in the long run, help stop terrorist attacks on Americans.

By contrast, most Europeans disapproved of the raid. In Great Britain 71 percent disagreed with Prime Minister Margaret Thatcher's decision to allow the American use of a British base. Chancellor Helmut Kohl of West Germany warned that the strike might provoke outbursts of "primitive anti-Americanism." There were other, better-reasoned arguments against the attack. Many asserted that it would only encourage further attacks, escalating the cycle of terror and revenge. Others argued the attack would worsen the strong anti-American feelings in the Middle East and ultimately rally new recruits to Qaddafi's cause. In the view of several

> ***That's what superpowers do.***
> —Libyan militiaman showing journalists the body of a child killed in the 1986 U.S. raid

European leaders, the United States was treating the symptoms, not the cause. Reprisals, they insisted, should be accompanied by concerted diplomatic efforts to bring about resolutions of Arab-Israeli conflicts, the Palestinian question, and other root causes of tension in the Middle East.

But in the months following the raid, instead of reinvigorating the peace process, the United States chose to apply psychological pressure on Qaddafi. In October 1986 an article by investigative reporter Bob Woodward in the *Washington Post* disclosed secret documents suggesting that the Reagan administration had engaged in a disinformation campaign to mislead the media — and hence Qaddafi — about American intentions. The campaign, according to a confidential memo by national security adviser John Poindexter, relied on a "series of closely coordinated events involving covert, diplomatic, military and public actions." The goal was to forestall further acts of terrorism by convincing Qaddafi that a second American air attack was imminent. Later in October, some Western nations began to reevaluate the assumption that Qaddafi was the Middle East's primary sponsor of terrorism. Attention shifted to Syria after the trial of suspected Jordanian terrorist Nezar Hindawi produced what

UPI/BETTMANN NEWSPHOTOS

Libyan militiamen bear a coffin to a Tripoli cemetery for burial. In the United States, a poll showed almost 70 percent popular approval of Reagan's action in bombing Libya, but abroad, only the British, Canadian, and Israeli governments supported the attack.

We are ready to die, and we are ready to carry on fighting and defending our country.
—MUAMMAR EL-QADDAFI

UPI/BETTMANN NEWSPHOTOS

Qaddafi at home in his goatskin tent with his daughter Aysha. Terrorist outrages continued to occur even after the U.S. raid on Libya. Other Muslim governments (Syria and Iran) are widely believed to sponsor and train terrorists. But Qaddafi remains the only head of state who openly embraces terrorism as a political tool.

Great Britain called "conclusive evidence" that Syria was behind Hindawi's attempt to blow up an Israeli airliner leaving London in April. While some European nations moved cautiously, seeing Syria as a key figure in the Middle East peace process, Great Britain severed its relations with Hafez al-Assad's country. For his part, Qaddafi, according to Israeli intelligence sources, continued to operate 20 terrorist camps in Libya, where he trained 7,000 people of various nationalities. He continued to see himself as an emissary of Allah sent to restore the Arabs to lost glory. In his distorted imagination, he fully expected to succeed in destroying Israel and in establishing his unique system of Arab socialism throughout the world. He also vowed to persist in confronting the United States. "It is too easy and simplistic to dismiss Qaddafi as mad," said a Western diplomat in Tripoli. "He genuinely believes that the cause is just so there's no deflecting him. He'll pursue his fight with the U.S. until he dies."

Further Reading

Anderson, Lisa. *The State and Social Transformation in Tunisia and Libya, 1830–1980.* Princeton, New Jersey: The Princeton University Press, 1986.

Aufderheide, Patricia. *Anwar Sadat.* New York: Chelsea House Publishers, 1985.

Behnke, Roy. *The Herders of Cyrenaica: Ecology, Economy and Kinship Among the Bedouin of Eastern Libya.* Urbana: University of Illinois Press, 1980.

Cooley, John K. *Libyan Sandstorm.* New York: Holt, Rinehart and Winston, 1982.

Deeb, Marius K. and Deeb, Mary Jane. *Libya Since the Revolution: Aspects of Social and Political Development.* New York: Praeger Publishers, 1982.

Haley, P. Edward. *Qaddafi and the United States Since 1969.* New York: Praeger Publishers, 1984.

Nelson, Harold D., ed. *Libya: A Country Study.* Washington, D.C.: Government Printing Office for Foreign Studies, the American University, 1979.

Qaddafi, Muammar el-. *The Green Book, Vol. I: The Solution of the Problem of Democracy.* London: Martin Brian and O'Keefe, 1976.

———. *The Green Book, Vol. II: The Solution of the Economic Problem.* London: Martin Brian and O'Keefe, 1978.

———. *The Green Book, Vol. III: The Social Basis of the Third Universal Theory.* Tripoli, Libya: Public Establishment for Publishing, Advertising and Distribution, 1978.

Wright, John L. *Libya: A Modern History.* Baltimore, Maryland: Johns Hopkins University Press, 1982.

Chronology

1942	Born Muammar el-Qaddafi in Libya's Sirtic Desert
Dec. 24, 1951	Libya becomes an independent nation under King Idris I
1956	Qaddafi organizes his first revolutionary group, a student organization dedicated to the overthrow of Idris
1963	Graduates from the University of Libya with a law degree
1965	Graduates from the Libyan Military College in Benghazi; is commissioned as a lieutenant in the army
Sept. 1, 1969	Overthrows King Idris and proclaims the formation of the Socialist Libyan Arab Republic
1970	Begins a campaign to finance international "independence movements"
	Removal of American and British military installations in Libya
Sept. 1970	Egyptian President Gamal Abdel Nasser dies and is succeeded by Anwar Sadat
April 17, 1971	Egypt, Libya, and Syria agree to form the Federation of Arab Republics, which dissolves two years later due to Egyptian-Libyan tensions
1972	Qaddafi sets up training camps for the National Arab Youth for the Liberation of Palestine (NAYLP)
April 15, 1973	Proclaims a "popular revolution" with a five-point reform program that includes arming citizens, purging political opponents, and promoting Islamic law
Sept. 1973	Nationalizes 51% of the assets of all foreign oil companies
July–Aug. 1977	War breaks out between Egypt and Libya
Aug. 19, 1981	American ships cross Qaddafi's "line of death" and enter the Gulf of Sidra; two Libyan warplanes are shot down
Oct. 6, 1981	Assassination of Egyptian President Anwar Sadat
March 24, 1986	U.S. Navy enters the Gulf of Sidra for a second time and sinks two Libyan patrol boats
April 4, 1986	A bomb explodes in a discotheque in Germany, wounding hundreds; U.S. intelligence sources implicate Qaddafi
April 14, 1986	The United States bombs Libya

Index

Benjamin Kyle is a New York-based freelance writer who has written on a variety of topics, especially Middle-Eastern politics and culture.

Arthur M. Schlesinger, jr., taught history at Harvard for many years and is currently Albert Schweitzer Professor of the Humanities at City University of New York. He is the author of numerous highly praised works in American history and has twice been awarded the Pulitzer Prize. He served in the White House as special assistant to Presidents Kennedy and Johnson.